Life Learned Abroad:

Lessons on Humanity from China

Brandon Ferdig

This book is dedicated to Grandpa Ferdig. As a boy, his gentle manner always made me feel secure and free to be me.

This book is dedicated to Grandpa Freyholtz for passing down his love and pursuit of knowledge and wisdom.

Contents:

Introduction

Our seated bodies stuttered as the plane touched down. I looked out my window seat—it was just an airport tarmac, yet it was surreal being on the ground someplace so new and different. A whole new energy rose within me and a clarity opened the door to the experiences and insights ahead.

I landed in China around 9:00 a.m. on Saturday, August 28, 2010. After seventeen hours and one layover traveling across the ocean into another hemisphere, I reached Guangzhou. I liked to do the math in my head: "If I left San Francisco at 1:00 a.m. and it's 9:00 a.m. now, but 8:00 p.m. back in Minnesota…" Somehow it worked out to where I left late at night and arrived in the morning. Sounds nice, except you are en route much longer than that time difference. So your body thinks it's supposed to be around 9:00 *p.m.* "Time to get ready for bed," your body tells you over breakfast. Jet lag's a trip.

Guangzhou, China's third largest city at 12.8 million people, sits on the north tip of the Pearl River Delta, a bay jutting into the mainland on China's southern coast.

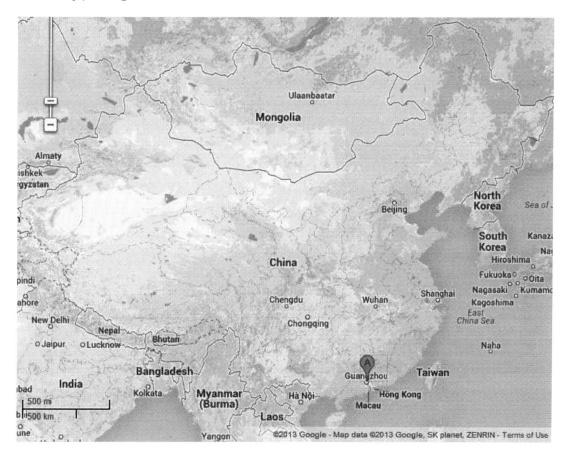

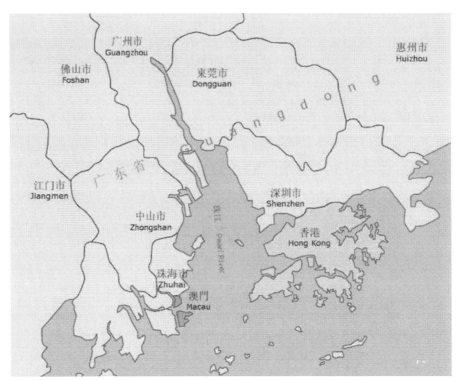

The Pearl River Delta, Guangdong Province: Guangzhou, the capital of Guangdong, is about seventy-five miles (121 km) northwest of Hong Kong. (wikimedia.org)

I unbuckled my seatbelt and watched all the Chinese passengers stand up. After a minute, I did as well, then grabbed my bags and made for the exit. I tunneled through to the terminal, and on the other side there they were. Chinese characters on a wall advertisement in their blockish, idiosyncratic, Far Eastern declaration.

The Guangzhou Baiyun International Airport terminal looked similar to that of any other large airport I've been in: neutral-colored corridors flanked by sit-down and fast food restaurants, convenience stores, newsstands, bench seating, and luggage carts. Yet all the visuals and noises decorating and filling the air radiated a palpable novelty, and the few things that did differ—the stick figure for the exit sign, foods available at the convenience shops—stuck out like the one picture hanging crookedly on your living room wall. Then there was the most obvious, expected, yet noteworthy element—the people. From the countless travelers to the coffee shop barista to the janitor, and from the baggage handlers driving the luggage transporters below on the tarmac to pilots and crew back in the plane, everyone was Chinese.

I looked out the large windows beyond the cars, planes, and runways and viewed the green, hilly landscape. Then it hit me good: that's *Chinese* soil. That far-off place we always (yet only) hear about on the news, and I'm here for the next eleven months. An emotional prism separated each feeling: anxiety, excitement, loneliness, and curiosity. But let's face it, one wonders if the degree of my emotion was a consequence of my upbringing. Back home in the United States, China is not just another foreign country like Germany or Mexico. China is the mysterious "East"—that monster of Communism. As a result, China has this other-worldly, celebrity status in America—though rarely the hero of the story.

As I walked along and pushed my luggage cart among the many other travelers, I did see a couple other Western businessmen. Nonetheless, within this social sphere I first felt the polar sensations of being invisible and obvious. I wasn't part of this new world; I was more of a fly on the wall. Yet unlike the tiny fly, my blonde head stuck out like a sore thumb. I opted for the invisible these first moments. To cross the line with a *Ni hao* (Chinese for "hello") to a passing stranger would be the declaration of my presence, inserting myself into their world. I wasn't sure how to dip my toe into those waters. So I just rolled my luggage along contentedly observing. Of course, crossing this line was as inevitable as my challenges with their language—both poking their heads up at the same time.

I approached a counter near the airport exit to see about getting a bus ticket to my final destination. I could say one word in Chinese: *Zhuhai*. The city I would call home. The lady on the other side of the counter said something back to me like "bla, bla, shengzhoumaleihoufengzhu."

Oh boy.

I handed her some denomination of money, and she gave me change and a ticket. I walked away thinking, "Okay, Brandon, if you're gonna experience this country, best to know a few more words."

I exited the auto-sliding double-doors with my bus ticket and bags. Along the sidewalk of the airport pickup drive, I saw a row of signs designating busing destinations. A few signs down read "Zhuhai." I handed my ticket to the girl dressed like a flight attendant waiting by the sign. She didn't react much, so I knew I was in the right line. Soon a bus pulled up. I put my luggage in its belly compartment, boarded, and got comfortable for the two-and-a-half hour ride southbound to Zhuhai.

***

I grew up in a town 700 people strong. (Go ahead and say it, "That's smaller than my high school!" I hear it quite a bit.) Blackduck, Minnesota is located an hour south of Canada. And to be accurate, I didn't even live in town. Rather, my father, mother, sister, three brothers, a dog, several cats, and I lived on thirty acres of woods and field.

Although we weren't without modern luxuries—we had snowmobiles and a motorboat, satellite TV and a PC—it was the spirit of the land that lived in our home. Mom had a big garden and clothesline, and the boys hunted and fished. Each spring we'd grab spears and drive to creeks to stab the sucker fish spawning upstream each season. When finding a school of fish, we'd walk through the creek in rolled-up jeans as these four-pound, carp-like fish squirmed and wiggled in our hands and darted between our legs. One time I came home, stripped to bathe, and found birthmarks all over my body. Uh oh, those weren't birthmarks but bloodsuckers.

We lived outside the urban and suburban norm of most America, away from just about everyone. But that didn't keep me from observing humans and nurturing my interest to understand one another. I first took note of the Native Americans in the region—the struggles within the Indian Reservations as well as the relations between them and the other Minnesotans. I also became interested in the individual experience. At seventeen I remember talking with my friend's grandmother one afternoon about being widowed. The topic was not uncomfortable, actually. The idea simply occurred to me of having been married for so many years and now having to go to bed alone each night. "Do you still talk to him?" I asked. Her eyes moistened as she shared how much she missed him.

After graduating high school, I moved to the Twin Cities to study psychology. Upon completion of my bachelor's degree at the University of Minnesota, I worked on campus for a psychological research study. But I realized I wasn't a lab guy or a counseling guy. I liked interviewing and observing people and learning their stories and experiences, so I moved toward journalism and media. By my mid-twenties I monkeyed with a cable access show in Minneapolis, interned for an Internet radio show, and started a blog—which changed names about five times. I was paying my bills by selling health insurance and felt like I was spinning my wheels in life. But I found traction when I hit the road—all it took was a trip to see my cousin in Boston.

I figured I would see The Windy City on the way, so I took a bus from Minneapolis to Chicago, where I would fly out to Boston. On the ride, I chatted it up with a twenty-something geeky-looking guy who was also on his way to Chicago and a plus-size woman in her thirties on her way to Cincinnati. I surprised myself by how alive with conversation I was with these two, but I had left all my troubles and concerns back at home. The relief of moving forward without the burdens of bills, relationships, and career prompted a release of expression with my two companions. Meanwhile, reading the book *Zen Mind, Beginner's Mind* from my bus seat was a powerful accompaniment. Be present in mind and body with each step you take as if each was in new territory, it said. That came easy as every mile traveled *was* new to me.

I exited the bus at downtown Chicago's Union Station terminal and walked the sidewalk in the pleasant fall afternoon. I felt like an alien arriving on Earth for the first time, my detached perspective making this new city/world so striking: the pedestrians, traffic, buildings. But I also felt a belonging as my unburdened presence made the city feel so accessible. Later this trip I experienced the "new world" of Boston, and in the following months and years there were many other domestic and international destinations—each a refreshed setting with an abundance of things to experience and people to befriend.

The openness of travel allowed not just increased interaction, but insight. About a year after Boston, I was in the small Guatemalan city of Panajachel on the coast of Lake Atitlan—a stunningly picturesque lake of blue waters surrounded by old mountains worn with enormous grooves that were completely covered in bright green vegetation. I took an old motorboat ride across the lake to an even smaller, more isolated village. After we docked, I walked along the boulder-strewn coast and was a bit embarrassed to find that the local women I approached doing laundry on the rocks were topless. Up the bank, I walked a snail's pace through the village and its outskirts which were just fifty yards away in any direction. I encountered a farmer with one pig that ate slop in its tiny, old wooden stall while the elderly man hoed the land leisurely. I'm not sure if there was a more civilized opposite to the rushed, pressured, pay-off-your-debt life that I knew in America. Yet until I experienced this contrast, I had a tough time conceiving of life outside such circumstances.

In addition to specific lessons learned in Guatemala was the general enjoyment of expanding my knowledge and wisdom of the world by immersing myself in foreign destinations. I knew that to continue growing meant my next step was to embark on more than a sampling of internationalism. I needed to stew in a global perspective. I needed to live abroad. I searched for work opportunities at foreign newspapers, with a businessman in Slovenia who I met in Thailand, and even modeling in China. Nothing developed. In the meantime, though, I was having an international experience domestically: tutoring three teenage siblings of a Somali refugee family in St. Paul. Though it wasn't my first choice, I realized that teaching English abroad was a good option. Then, in March 2010, I met a young gentleman named Joe at my salsa dance class. Joe had recently returned from teaching English in a city in China called Zhuhai. He introduced me to his contact there. After a few emails and a phone interview, they offered me a job.

However, I drafted acceptance and denial emails. I worried this endeavor was putting off "real life"—career, finances, relationships. Mom, who had already protested her son visiting Malaysia the year before and missing Christmas, was even more against me being gone a whole year. Indeed, I'd be her only child outside Minnesota. Tipping the scale, though, was my mild-mannered friend, Paul. We were hanging out that spring when I shared my indecision. In his usual calm and collected manner, he replied, "Brandon, you'd be a fool not to go."

I reconsidered all the reasons to leave and realized any serious attempt to understand the world necessitated cultural immersion—particularly in one as pronounced as China's. Ten days after they offered me a job, I sent the acceptance email. A couple months later, my visa arrived. I was going to live in China.

***

By living abroad, I gained even more of an appreciation for the lives of the culture in which I was immersed. Also, by comparison, I gained an enhanced clarity with which to understand the people and ways of my home country. Finally, this unique setting offered a reset and reexamination of all general notions of what it means to be human, addressing topics such as education, relationships, poverty, freedom, and more. This is what this book is about.

To start off, I acquaint you with life in China: my neighborhood, city, job, colleagues, and routine (chapters 1-4). After adjusting to life half a world away, I share stories from my year that reveal lessons and themes (chapters 5-13). Finally, I take you along as I travel central China over the three weeks to end my year (chapters 14-18).

While reading this book, you'll see many pictures—particularly with the scenic locations. Take your time with the images. It'll help you be in each place I write about and improve the flow of the story.

Whether a morning visiting a fish market, an afternoon photographing a protest, or a day touring a Chinese factory; whether teaching local children or going on a date with a local woman; whether staying in quiet rural villages or surveying historic metropolises, I hope you find this book to be educational, emotive, intriguing, and most of all, enjoyable.

PART 1: A Whole New World

Chapter One: The Arrival

We know it as China. But that's not what they call it. They say: *Zhōng guó* (中国). We Westerners can thank 1300s Italian explorer Marco Polo for our label of this nation. The Chinese originate their name in its meaning: Middle Nation.

[Zhōng guó is an example of pinyin: Western lettering of the Chinese characters. You'll continue to see pinyin throughout this book, but no need to be discouraged or confused. After all, Beijing (Běijīng, 北京) and Shanghai (Shànghǎi, 上海) are familiar examples of pinyin. So are the two cities I've already mentioned: Guangzhou (Guǎngzhōu, 广州) and Zhuhai (Zhūhǎi, 珠海), my home town in China, which is pronounced "jew hi" and means pearl of the sea. *The accent marks, which are neglected with common examples of pinyin, indicate one of the four tones in Mandarin Chinese.]*

China is enormous, smaller only than Canada and Russia. It now has the world's second-largest economy, recently passing Germany and Japan. Still, people's incomes average only around $5,000 a year as the impressive total economic numbers are explained by China's massive population—they rank number one in the world in this category. Thus, the magnificence of skylines and development of metropolises like Shanghai and Hong Kong are offset by poverty in much of rural—and urban—China. This contrast was evident immediately on my two-and-a-half hour bus ride south from the Guangzhou airport to my new home, Zhuhai.

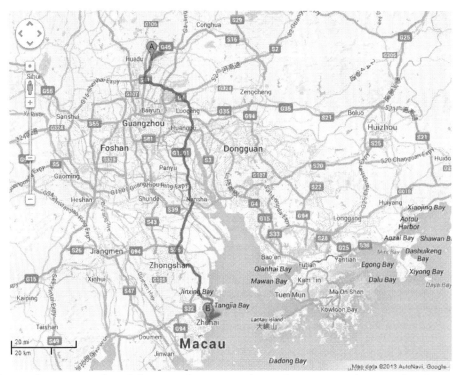

Zhuhai lies along the west side of the Pearl River Delta adjacent to the north of Macau and across the water from the islands of Hong Kong.

On the bus, I enjoyed the luxury of two seats to myself on the right side (passenger's side in China). I assumed the window seat, eyes affixed outside on the cars, billboards, and landscapes. Leaving the airport and city behind, we drove by lush, green hills separated by lakes of farmland. Grey skies did cover the horizon—smog or clouds, I did not know—which made it a gloomier scene.

More prominent than the natural element, though, was the human one. From the elevated freeway I viewed cranes and bulldozers sprinkled amongst infrastructure developments: roads, bridges, and buildings. All the while, these structures and projects were surrounded by humble farmsteads. I watched a farmer wearing a conical hat with a couple cattle, a few acres, and a lot of work to be done by hand amidst the backdrop of a factory in the distance.

China: first/third world intersection

At this point on the bus ride, my focus turned inward. A biological battle of fatigue versus excitement was in the balance—and favoring the former as minutes ticked by. Meanwhile, I was in need of a phone so I could call the woman who was to pick me up at the bus stop in Zhuhai. I saw a lady sitting across the aisle. If this was that bus ride to Chicago, I would have been happy for the excuse to reach out and ask a stranger for help despite the language barrier, which didn't prevent such interactions in other foreign countries I had traveled. But beyond being fatigued, I was uptight and uneasy asking if I could use her phone. She even knew some English and was very kind to walk up to the front and give her phone to the driver to listen to instructions about where to drop me off. Nonetheless, I was anxious and uncomfortable—and confused as to why. But I think even in these first moments, the excitement of travel was tempered by the reality that this wasn't just a vacation. I was here to live.

Eventually, hills, bridges, and farmsteads gave way to residential developments and businesses. In the early afternoon the bus came to a stop, and the driver turned and said something to me. Prompted to look outside, I was relieved to see a small, brown car with "TPR English" written on the side. A woman of about thirty greeted me in English as I exited the bus. Eva, the English name of the school employee in charge of teacher relations, had wavy, shoulder-length black hair and a natural smile, which she had the habit of covering with her hand. Over the next week or so, Eva would take me to the bank to set up an account, to the clinic to pass my physical examination (necessary for work visa), and then to the visa center itself. These next few hours, however, of riding around, seeing my school offices, and getting my apartment, are a blur. Having just four hours of sleep over a thirty-eight-hour stretch, I was out like a light by 6:00 p.m.

Zzzzzzzzzzzzz

I awoke in my bed and did one of those looks back and forth where the head stays put but the eyes dart. I heard loud Chinese conversation below my window.

"Oh that's right," I remembered.

Though it was early morning, I got up with afternoon alertness. (Ah, the upside of jet lag.) I walked out of my bedroom and looked around. White walls and smooth, off-white, large-tiled floors covered the entrance, dining/living area, and both bedrooms. Between the bedrooms, the bathroom had grubbier, gray, ceramic mini-tiles—*and a Western toilet.* (This opposed the hole-in-the-floor alternative common in China.) There was no tub; the shower area was the rear of the bathroom with shower head that sprayed directly onto the floor. Straight ahead in the dining room was an off-white, glass-topped table. To the right in the living room, was an off-white couch and tan television stand with a twenty-five-inch tube TV atop. Then to the left, the kitchen had metal cupboards and a dishwasher where the oven "should've" been (below the cooking range), with no oven to be had at all.

Along the back living room wall was a sliding glass door leading to a deck/laundry space. To launder clothes in these parts, we had to wash them outside in the machine and let them drip-dry, hanging on the metal cage around our third-floor deck.

Apartments house the vast majority of residents in Zhuhai—in any given city in China, I imagine. Overall, I was pleased with this apartment. Teaching English abroad isn't a labor of luxury. My place was tidy and had everything I needed—-except heat, I'd find out.

I was eager to get outside. Like Dorothy landing in Oz? Not quite. Though leaving me a little woozy, my flight over here wasn't as dramatic as hers. Nor was China as colorful as Oz. Nonetheless, it was a whole new world. And this first day provided a succinct preview of the sights, sounds, experiences, and insights of my year.

I stepped out in shorts and a tee shirt to greet the warm morning. A concrete jungle lay before me: this complex of four or five twenty-story buildings surrounded the parking platform I walked along. We residents of this apartment village were in an urban island away from the grittier, noisier blocks surrounding us.

I walked by the old, wooden security desk that was manned by a teenager security guard dressed in navy blue pants, a light blue button-up shirt with a patch sewn on his shoulder, and a belt with a flashlight attached. For some reason their blue baseball caps had such oddly large brims. He paid me a wide, genuine smile—a reassuring way to begin my exposure to the locals. His innocent and smooth face, though, appeared quite non-threatening should things ever get dicey. But as I was to discover all year, "diceyness" just didn't occur, and the best examples I would have of people getting out of hand came from Westerners—once when a group of them at the bar were playing a game of *dice*, interestingly.

Just past the security desk, I took the outdoor stairway leading down to the street. While descending, the sights and sounds of residents playing ping-pong rose. At the bottom of the stairs, underneath the shade of the platform, two men guarded their space and swiped their arms with a ball darting between them.

I leaned against a pillar and watched. Here was my invisibility, and I liked it—not wanting their action to alter one iota, just a fly on the wall watching this slice of life in China. Soon enough, though, my obviousness got their attention and got me to do something less studious but more fun and memorable: participate. One gentleman ping-ponger motioned me to come join.

"Oh, well, I..." My Chinese as bad as the day prior, I nonetheless was happy to accept.

I'm not a good player, but I can be quick. But if I was quick, he was lightning, and you don't have to speak Chinese to understand what "HEYOWAA!" meant as he smoked one by me.

Ping-pong diplomacy on day one

After a handful of volleys, I gave them a *xiè xie* (谢谢)—Mandarin for "thank you." By then I had learned that much Chinese. Then I walked out the driveway and along the street.

***

My Neighborhood

The two main differences between this neighborhood in China and its American urban counterpart were its unkemptness and increased social energy.

I swung a left outside our complex and looked about wide-eyed. *Real China!* I lived in the old downtown of Zhuhai in the neighborhood called Xiangzhou (*xiāng zhōu*, 香洲). Back when fishing drove the economy—before the days of the developments in southern Zhuhai—this was the center of the city's attention. It retained an authentic, weathered, and cultured charm. Big, old trees grew through square openings in the sidewalks—their canopy adding a homeyness. Underneath, I walked through the warm, humid air along with other locals. The narrow streets had motorbikes and automobiles rolling by, around, and sometimes almost through the walkers. But it wasn't threatening. Things just flowed together.

The residential and the commercial also intermingled. Food and knick-knack vendors dressed the sidewalks and embodied the spirit of this neighborhood: approachable, unguarded, and genuine—these traits worn into their fashion and friendly faces. Small businesses occupied the ground floors of apartment buildings—most much smaller than my home complex.

And when referring to small business, I mean small. Some resembled little more than storage units with merchandise: ten feet wide, twenty feet deep, and three-walled as they had garage door-like entrances. These could be restaurants, clothing stores, liquor/cigarettes stores, stationery stores, electronics stores, DVD stores, and others I'm probably forgetting. Some parents had their preschool-aged children with them at their small shop or restaurant. Locals had no problem communicating with one another from opposite sides of the street, whether because they had to or because it was simply easier to yell. That level of familiarity and leisure among the residents reminded me of small-town America. Only this was a city.

Street mechanics working on starters

Store workers working on beauty sleep

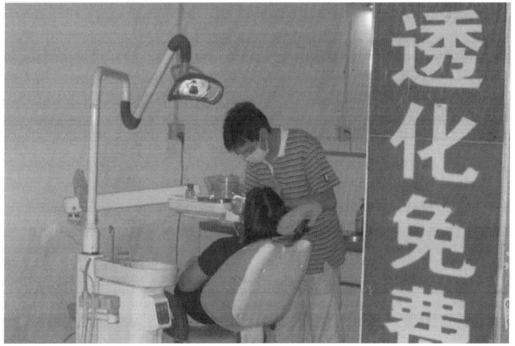

"Open up and say, 'Cheese.'"

Looking around and wondering where to wander, I recalled our drive the day before going along the coast. I walked in the direction I thought we had come from and discovered that my apartment was only three blocks from the ocean. It wasn't all beaches and cream. Two opposing dimensions of Zhuhai were revealed simultaneously: natural beauty and pollution. Zhuhai is known for its healthy environmental practices, even garnering some international recognition over the years. I discovered evidence for this distinction hugging the ocean—a boulevard with a bike trail and bricked sidewalk within the larger, grassy corridor wrapping the bay in palm trees, hedges, and sculpture.

This beauty contrasted the "real," if not grimy, aspects behind this coastal façade. I turned around and approached the docks.

And then from looking up and back toward the city, to looking down and toward the water, a 180-degree change in view also meant a 180-degree change in aesthetics.

In addition, just into the water I saw a band 5-10 feet wide (1.5-3 meters) of floating debris—Styrofoam, plastic, wrappers, and grey-brown gunk—bobbing with the waves and extending for a hundred yards or more down the coast. Nature was kind to accumulate this rubbish into a row. It seemed all one might have to do to collect it would be to stick a huge net into the water alongside a boat as it drove along the litter line. But the decoration stayed all year.

Dozens of fishing boats lined the docks. Some appeared quite luxurious, while others I couldn't believe were buoyant.

Some were 20 feet (6 meters) long; others were upwards of 60 (18.25 meters). All had the Chinese flag.

The four smaller stars originally represented the four social classes. That is not official any longer. But what is, is what the big star has always stood for since the flag's creation: the Chinese Communist Party (CCP).

Along with the boats tied to the docks were dozens more anchored in rows a hundred yards or more out into the bay.

Lovely island behind it

I walked out onto the docks which housed a subculture within this already-novel Zhuhai culture. Mostly younger men—but also some women—chatted, cleaned, organized nets, drank soda, and smoked cigarettes often all at the same time. Some walked up and down from dock to land carrying odds and ends, talking loudly with the others doing the same. On one dock, a lady set up a little table and cooler selling snacks and drinks. It was a community unto itself.

I sensed this wasn't just a static scene I saw before me, but included a depth and richness of a lifestyle going back generations.

I made eye contact with a middle-aged guy all alone in his small boat tied to the dock. He somehow communicated to me the opportunity to go for a ride around the bay. I knew not to accept his first price, but took his second. So I'm sure he ended up taking me in more ways than one. I jumped in, and he started the loud, rattling engine. We roared around the bay and got a closer look at the boats.

That's a lot of net.

I saw some fishermen lounging on the decks of their boats. I was surprised to see one foursome of young men hanging out in nothing but their tighty-whities. Athletic as they were, I didn't take fishermen as the kind of guys who'd be so free with their three-quartered nakedness.

Turns out my driver gave rides to fishermen like these whose boats were anchored offshore. So he killed two birds with one stone and picked up a few fully-clothed fishermen before bringing us all back to shore.

I walked the docks back to land and caught a fisherman catching a catch in a style I'd never seen.

The rope in his right hand connected to the top of a four-pole pyramid. At its base was a large square net. Every so often he'd pull the rope, raising the pyramid out of the water to reveal fishes flopping in the net.

I continued on to new blocks of my neighborhood, taking in the midday buzz of the same residential/commercial blend. Another evident blend was that which I first noticed in the countryside: first/third world lifestyles. From looking back at the bright white high-rises along the coast, I walked the side streets and alleys where people in old clothing rode rusty bicycles, ate at humble eateries, and offered one-man services such as cobbling or knife sharpening.

It was hot out. I'd find that coming from the comforts of air-conditioning, afternoons in August felt like taking a lid off of a pot of hot water and getting a face full of steam. I got used to it, but in the beginning my slippery back was annoying. On top of being warm, I was lost. Everything being so different from Minneapolis meant nothing stood out to help mark my way. It was funny, then, how the energy of markets and motorbikes and street mechanics that I enjoyed in the morning was now tiring and even jarring with each horn honk or person yelling. It seems if you're not up to riding a social energy wave, it'll take you under.

Wandering the back blocks in need of directions, my invisibility frustrated me. I was turned down a couple times when handing a Zhuhai street map to locals. One shop owner standing near his entrance waved his hands in a rejection gesture after just glancing at it. I thought, "How can you not know where we are? You live here and the map is in Chinese!"

I decided to do something about this heat. I visited one of the tiny convenience vendors on a corner and bought an iced tea. I wondered how these retailers made ends meet; but evidently they had business, because he pulled out and rifled through a cardboard box full of crumpled, mixed bills to make change.

*[Chinese money can be called either the yuan or RMB, short for renmibi (rénmínbì, 人民币). Technically, the yuan is the **unit** of the renminbi. We don't have that distinction in the United States as the dollar is the name of the currency and the unit. One RMB is worth about $.15. One US dollar is about 6.1RMB.]*

100RMB is worth about $15.90.

I guzzled down the tea. Then I looked for a trash can. Finding none, I asked a group of young guys sitting on some nearby steps by indicating my empty bottle and shrugging my shoulders. One gestured his own response: a back-handed flick. Without breaking eye contact, I followed his lead. *Flick.* The bottle spun head over heels in the air before landing a hollow-sounding "donk, dunk, te." I turned to see the bottle come to a rolling stop on the sidewalk, looked back to him, and he to me with a nod.

When in Rome.

While still lost and wandering, I looked up and out beyond the nearby buildings when I noticed a large "TPR" displayed on the top floor of a distant four-story commercial building. I recognized it from the day before as the headquarters of my school. I was relieved to now have somewhere to go. (Later I'd wonder how I got lost. After just a couple days being here, the route to the school was second nature. How quickly we become familiar with our surroundings; how funny how lost we are when new.)

I approached, entered, and introduced myself to the receptionist at the front desk.

Eva, the woman who picked me up from the bus stop, came down from her office and took me out for lunch. In the alley behind the school, we walked into a small eatery, a white-tiled space no larger than a living room. I looked around and ordered what appeared tasty on someone else's plate before sitting on a plastic chair at one of the eight metal rectangular tables. As the food came out, I asked about water. Eva kindly retorted that we had soup for beverage. Still, I repeated my request—apparently one not commonly made. The waitress went to the back and brought out an eight ounce Dixie cup of warm water. Interesting. But it did the trick. Next I searched for a napkin. Observing me look around the table, Eva explained that we are supposed to come with our own. BYON, I guess. Eva asked our waitress, who brought out a packet for sale for one yuan. They were adorned with some famed, cartoon sheep.

Something about the combination of a small cup of warm water and cartoon napkins—and their amusing clash with life as I knew it—had me emit a chuckle.

I knew I'd have to get used to how things were done here, but it was also very apparent how China had succumbed to outside influence. One of the first things that caught my eye was that license plates had Arabic numerals rather than Chinese characters. I saw a "4" rather than a "四"; a "7" rather than a "七". Not surprising, much of the clothing worn here had been assumed from the Western style, and also it was not rare to find English written on them. And with English came English misspellings.

Jsut do it?

After we finished eating, Eva had to get back to work, and I decided to get back to my apartment. By this time (mid-afternoon), my body was telling me it was three o'clock in the morning. So I had the idea to lie down and watch some DVDs. I didn't pack any, though, so had to find some to buy. On my way back, I approached the neighborhood department store, Jusco.

Groggily walking the department store aisles, I heard another Western influence: American pop music from the 1980s playing overhead and alternating with Chinese pop songs. All they had for American films were lousy B-movies with Chinese subtitles or, in case I was interested in testing my Mandarin, loudly voiced-over Chinese actors speaking the roles. I bought a couple.

Almost back to my building, one last Western import with a Chinese twist made for a fitting finale. Right along the sidewalk just outside a liquor/cigarette store was one of those arcade/vending machines that require the user to direct a claw over the desired item, hit a button, and then hope that the claw grasps and retrieves it. Two teenage boys prepared to play on this machine. It looked the same as any of the countless versions we've all seen but for two things—the cartoon characters that adorned it (that popular cartoon sheep again), and the merchandise within.

Inside were three things: bags of chips, cans of something, and packs of cigarettes. And these boys weren't hungry.

The guys giggled as the claw lightly took hold of a pack and lifted it a few inches, but then sighed with frustration as gravity had other ideas.

Right after this shot I put down my camera, and just my luck (and just theirs) I missed the chance to record them as they actually won a pack on the very next try. They, of course, were elated at their bargain smokes.

I was struck by this relaxed legal policy, but it did seem a fitting accompaniment to the informal, comfortable social code of my neighborhood (which struck me as well). The whole lack of rigidity here clashed with my presumptions because this was supposed to be anti-freedom Communist China. I learned this day that freedom is more than a policy—it's a feeling. The leisurely feel of my neighborhood was very freeing. Regarding policy, I realized that the concept of "freedom in China" would also depend on what part of China is being addressed. Here were these boys playing an arcade game for cigarettes. I saw cars driving (and parked) in ways that would entice tickets in Minneapolis. I saw people walking in the street with an open can of beer—also illegal in my home city. In the coming days, however, I would encounter the well-known nationwide restrictions (mainly, Internet censorship). The top-down social order seemed to counterbalance the lack of legal enforcement at the neighborhood level.

I learned right away in my year that freedom is a malleable, multi-definable notion experienced from different recipes in different societies.

***

After the arcade game antics I went back to my apartment and watched one of those B-movies before going to bed in an effort to recalibrate my body clock.

Chapter Two: Getting Acquainted

Throughout this first week, I explored other neighborhoods in Zhuhai, became further acquainted with the ways of life here, and got to know a few fellow teachers. Then I was thrown onstage in a drastic flip from invisible observer to obvious participant.

Heath and Gongbei

I shared my apartment with another teacher. His name was Heath, an Australian a couple years shy of me but taller and bigger with a gregarious personality to match. He had dark, buzzed hair and a great smile on his face which often emitted an exuberant, rhythmic bellow. He partied late, drank a lot of Chinese beer, and chased Chinese women. Heath had been in Zhuhai about six months when I arrived, and the second day after I landed, he decided to show me around.

We left on another warm, sunny day in shorts and short sleeves and hopped aboard a bus southbound to the neighborhood of Gongbei (*Gǒngběi*, 拱北).

Our neighborhood, Xiangzhou, had the city roots. Jida (Jídà, 吉大) had banking, business, and expensive residences. Gongbei, though, was about entertainment, shopping, and people-watching.

Gongbei's biggest boon was its border with Macau—the wealthy autonomous region adjacent south of Zhuhai. This meant the many tourists, workers, students, and others who used the Zhuhai-to-Macau Bordergate came through this neighborhood; and *this* meant hotels, restaurants, clubs, and shopping malls for Gongbei.

Gongbei's most notable entertainment area was *Shui Wan* or "Bar Street," a row of colorful nightclubs packed each weekend with young people dressed to impress, the loud beats stirring them up. Heath and I didn't take in the night life on this daytrip, but we did investigate the always-energized Walking Street, another well-known stroll in Gongbei. As its name suggests, it is a pedestrian-only road with restaurants, shopping, and even massage if you're up for it. (If interested, don't worry about having to search out the massage places. Their people will approach you.)

Walking street at night.

In between the out-front-and-shiny features of Gongbei were the rougher and raw innards of small streets and alleys. Heath found these more interesting. Initially walking along a main road where our bus dropped us off, Heath darted off into the alleys as I followed along. With six months' familiarity, he knifed through narrowing alleyways past countless vendors lining the way who offered anything from peanuts to umbrellas to houseplants to pet fish and pet birds to...*showbiz monkeys?*

The monkey handler demanded coin for a picture despite its protestations to hold onto Heath's fingers.

The monkey was just a bonus that neither Heath, nor certainly I, had anticipated. There was actually another animal Heath was on his way to show me. Moving along, we popped out into an alley crossway. Heath walked over to a corner stall where, out front, two young guys with rubber boots over their blue jeans kept busy with customers and product preparation. When they saw Heath and me approach, they grinned and stepped back to make room for the attraction, or product, they knew we came for.

This was the "before" shot.

Out along the front of the stall was the post-preparatory offering for customers:

From the grimy to the hip, and from above the ground to below, Heath then took me to Gongbei's largest, most popular shopping destination, The Underground Market (as we English-speakers called it). So-called for obvious reasons, the fact that it was built down rather than up didn't hinder its size. The Underground Market was a maze of broad and narrow corridors with over a hundred tiny-to-small independent operations selling everything from toys to jewelry to clothes to electronics to sporting goods to dirty movies.

I didn't shop this day—just walked through and took in all the activity. I'd be back, though.

After getting lost underground, and then finding our way out, Heath and I returned to our bus stop on the main road. Here, Gongbei gave us one last character to see us off: a young gentleman who played guitar on his head for donations.

It was my first of many trips to Gongbei—for work and play—and the first of a few excursions those initial days.

***

Coasting Down the Coast with Marilyn

My colleague Marilyn agreed to join me to venture down the coast. And while walking was the obvious means to traverse the lovely boulevard, we decided to give another mode of transportation a try.

I met Marilyn the following day at the school. She was from the Philippines, though her English was so natural you'd think it was her mother tongue. She was a petite woman with golden skin and smooth black hair. She also had a big smile and liked to show it. With her fun-loving spirit, she thought it a good idea to rent one of those double bicycles. We covered a good amount of ground while retaining the intimacy with our new surroundings that automobile travel lacks.

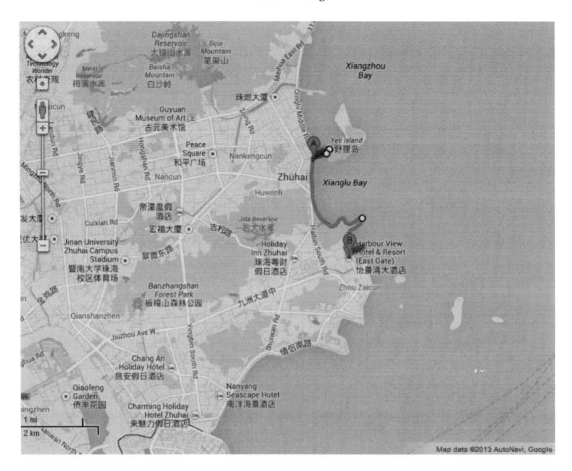

A couple bike rental guys and a lady selling sugarcane to chew set up shop at the foot of the bridge going out to an island called Yeli Dao (*Yě li dǎo*, 野狸岛), just off the coastline of my neighborhood. We picked out the best bike, but it was still an old, paint-chipped contraption with narrow-set handle bars, rattling pedals, and an unreliable bike-bell—the kind you press and makes that cash-register "ch-ching" sound. Because she feared tanning, Marilyn was covered head-to-toe in jeans, a corduroy button-up shirt, and an ear-flapped cap in the heat of South China September. So, in this land of 99% Chinese people, a lanky white guy and a bundled-up Filipina started off across the third-mile-long bridge to Yeli Dao.

Maneuvering along the sidewalk of this automobile bridge required increased control from me, the driver. Stopping and starting involved moments of tipsy, drunken-like biking skill. Learning to ride this two-seater was similar to learning to ride a single-seater as a child. We pedaled along in complete lack of style and form, but the function was all we cared about. We wobbled along, enjoying one of those spur-of-the-moment decisions you'd probably talk yourself out of if proposed back home.

On the other side of the bridge, an inviting boulder welcomed us to pose.

"Ye li dao"

Then I turned the tables and took a picture of those who took ours. We weren't the only ones here to enjoy the island.

Marilyn was well-protected with clothes. Chinese women liked to stay pale with umbrellas.

Yeli Dao was maybe a mile-and-a-half around, with a skirt of rocks and coarse sand surrounding the large, lush green island mound. There is actually something like a hundred islands of varying size that belong to Zhuhai and dot the horizon of the South China Sea.

We started our circumnavigation.

Fishing boats on the horizon

Making our way around and right back across the bridge to where we started, we then took the lovely coastal boulevard bike path southbound. Though beautiful, our cruise was regularly interrupted with curbs, large rocks, and traffic when the path sort of just narrowed off, at which point we had to ride the shoulder of the busy coastal road. So early on in our arrival to China, though, such inconveniences were quaint. The next stop on our dandy tandem was the Zhuhai Fisher Girl Statue.

From Virtualtourist.com: "Zhuhai Fisher Girl Statue is the landmark of the city. Standing elegantly at Xianglu Bay, she drapes a fishnet and holds a pearl high in the air with both hands up to the sky. The statue symbolizes a vigorous and lively Zhuhai welcoming visitors from all over the world."

There were many large boulders jutting out of the water besides the one the Fisher Girl was atop. One could play hopscotch out into the bay as others there did, but Marilyn and I stayed on the concrete-and-stone walkway, as did this guy who greeted us:

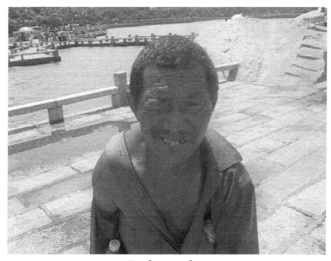

Seeking alms

After a fill of the Fisher girl, we saddled up. Marilyn and I peddled south around that finger of land and into the Jida neighborhood. Around the bend, an impressive white and glass-sided building came into sight to our right.

A little further up was a complex of several businesses, one of which was "Roman Seaside Restaurant."

We entered the spotless space, found a comfortable, padded booth, and enjoyed the air-conditioning and a glass of (cold) water. It was a welcome break from the usual eateries around my apartment.

The owner approached—an American all right—a large, muscular, middle-aged Texan with military-cropped hair named Jim.

"How you liking China?" he asked us.

"Fine," I replied, "but my body's still adjusting to the food."

"Well, try this," said Jim and handed us a menu featuring a split of American and Chinese cuisines.

I ordered the lunch combo special: Chinese chicken, scallops, and spaghetti. This restaurant— perched upon the second story—featured an interesting view back toward the coastal road.

This parking lot was spiced up a bit with Communist China's historic leader, Mao Zedong's, private jet as an ornament.

A beach opened up straight across from this lot. Marilyn and I thought it would be a nice idea to walk it after lunch. It looked attractive as we approached.

Like the coast in my neighborhood, though, there was a deceptive beauty to it. You'll notice it's pretty empty. The sand was coarse and the water dirty. I never saw more than a handful of swimmers here all year.

One beachgoer seemed to have more the idea of what to do.

This was the southern-most point on our effortful bike ride. But rather than going straight back, we recalled the impossible-not-to-notice gigantic, bedroom-sized boulders along the coastal road just past the Fisher Girl statue. So on our return, we stopped to scale these supersized rocks.

Evidently, rocks have a lot to say in these parts.

This one eternally states "te qu hun" or "Soul Zone."

***

White Men Onstage

A day or two later our school reached out to Heath and me, asking us teachers to participate in a community celebration. Despite having gotten to know Heath and Marilyn and getting a little out and about, I still had been stewing in some awkwardness and discomfort settling into this foreign land. So when TPR reached out I agreed hoping to find a social groove out of the deal.

This "deal" was the thirty-year anniversary of the government's designation of Zhuhai as a Special Economic Zone (SEZ). Though not sexy, it is an important distinction as it was a big reason Zhuhai was a growing, international city—and thus offered expanded opportunities and experiences for me all year. Specifically, SEZ status grants Zhuhai economic incentives that lure international manufacturers. Shenzhen, another nearby SEZ-designated city, has grown famously to a degree that makes Zhuhai look paltry. Nonetheless, Zhuhai's transformation over the last twenty years has also been notable, morphing from a sleepy fishing city of tens of thousands to a manufacturing base of a million—certainly a reason to celebrate, as I found the Chinese love to do for anything involving their land.

The event was held on one of Zhuhai's city squares. There were a few such squares around town: large, stone-surfaced spaces with restaurants and retail surrounding them. This particular square was special as it had a large stage. Plus, a branch of our school was one of the surrounding businesses. Another cause for involvement, I'd discover, was that my school's founder had influential familial roots in Zhuhai and organized many community-wide events himself—which, like Zhuhai being an SEZ, created opportunities I was able to experience.

Heath and I arrived at the square on this late Thursday afternoon to rehearse for the evening's performance. We were joined by only one other teacher: a sixty-year-old, dark-haired, medium-built, mustached upstate New Yorker named John. I wondered why more of the thirty-five or so other teachers didn't come. Around us in the square were all these groups in matching, ornate costumes working on their routines. We three were just sort of left there not knowing what we were supposed to do, so we just watched.

When the time came, an organizer led us behind stage, and on the way informed us we'd be dancing. Dancing? I hardly had time to look confused. As soon as we were placed just off stage right, a cheesy techno beat blared, and she said to us, "Go!" Out we went on an enormous stage in our street clothes where the only thing louder than the music was my self-consciousness. And this was just rehearsal.

I remember all the room I had around me. And I didn't know if I should act silly or try to seriously dance.

After a minute of half-hearted dancing, the music stopped, and we gladly jumped offstage to make way for a choreographed group of uniformed dancers.

"What was that?" I asked Heath.

"I don't know, mate."

After rehearsal we went out for dinner and, after dusk, returned for show time.

The celebration started off with a pair of thirty-something male emcees making the audience of about 300 laugh before and between performances. The first performance was introduced: a group of twenty men and women, dressed ornately in bright yellow and reds, danced joyously while fifteen blue-clad women did a routine with drums attached to their midriffs. It all made me wonder even more what to make of our scrappy involvement.

Expressive

Legendary

Lovely

Soon, we were backstage again and told to go out and dance.

"How?" I asked this time.

"Just dance," the organizer told me.

"What does this have to do with Zhuhai's anniversary?"

"Have fun!" she eagerly responded.

As a performer I wanted my motivation. I didn't get it. And accompanying—more like replacing—the "social groove" I had sought was an amped-up awkwardness of being a spectacle. They say the best way to learn to swim is to just jump in. I give myself credit for that.

Audience happily looking on

To this day I don't know why they had us up there; I'll chalk it up to cultural differences. After we finished, I asked Sally, a twenty-eight-year-old TPR office employee, why we were asked to go up there.

"No purpose. Just for fun," she said. After a few seconds she added, "Don't worry, it's legal."

***

These first several days were exploratory, eventful, educational, and exposing. We wrap up this introduction with a few more shots of my new home.

Squid and shrimp: each drying in the sun and aromatizing the Xiangzhou sidewalks.

I never got used to the smell. But I preferred fish to trash.

One of the trees in my neighborhood "fertilized" on a weekend night; a cleaning person would come by to collect.

How about something a little more warm and fuzzy?

Along Walking Street in Gongbei

Along a sidewalk near my apartment

In the quiet neighborhood in northern Zhuhai, Tangjia (*Táng jiā*, 唐家), I heard a crunching in the shrubbery right next to the bus stop. There were chickens in this thicket. I don't know what kept these birds from flying away; I don't know who could claim them (or who couldn't claim them). I never saw a fence. One was pecking at anything, trying to dig up some food in the dry, patchy Earth to go along with his patchy feathers.

Back in my neighborhood, we go from cage free to...

One down on the bench. Fifty to go.

Now on to some people.

School's out!

Children not only walked home from school comfortably by themselves, but spent days off out playing with friends.

I spotted these guys looking for minnows in the city aqueduct.

Reservoir in the background

Lots of kids, but not many siblings.

This mural along a building wall near a school says, "In order for the country to be wealthy, and family to be a happy family, please control birth."

Representing the other side of life, I came across some gravestones.

Old cemetery in Tangjia

Finally, at my first group dining experience the night of the Zhuhai SEZ celebration, I was introduced to a cuisine novelty.

***

After dipping my toes, it was now time to get my feet wet. Moved forward by my involvement, I changed my tune to a frequency that dug a little deeper into life here.

Chapter Three: Getting Schooled

From exploration to education, I learned a lot about my job both in preparation and in class.

Education on Education

Oh that's right. I'm here to teach. Funny how this "detail" got lost in the whole mix. But it was no accident. I didn't want to think too much about teaching English because, honestly, I didn't think too much of it. Tons of others before me had gone abroad to teach. So what was the big deal? Plus, how hard could it be? Especially to a bunch of Chinese children who were going to be little soldier students. Thus, leading up to my departure, and despite all the encouragement I received, I was a little sheepish about admitting my job. I would say to others, "That's right, I'm going to China to write . . . oh, and teach."

Skip ahead, and here I was sitting in teacher training. And it was maybe one whole hour into it when I realized I had underestimated three things: the difficulty of doing this job well, how important a job it was, and how rewarding this experience would be.

My first-year colleagues and I gathered for teacher training in a classroom that—with the white board, map, and bulletin board—reminded me of any classroom in most any school back home. I sat in one of the twenty dark-blue plastic chairs with attached, dark-blue plastic desks. My colleagues included an Oregonian named Reynold, Marilyn, an Australian woman, an Englishman, and a Scotsman all ranging from late-twenties to mid-forties.

The Scot, the Englishman, and the Aussie sitting in the lobby awaiting training.

Soon, a middle-aged Iranian man in slacks and a white turtleneck walked in. He was tall and thin, clean-shaven, and had a receding hairline and smiling face. His name was Navid (sounds like "NahVEED"), and he was the education supervisor at TPR Academy of American English in Zhuhai. TPR is an acronym for Total Physical Response—a system of movement teaching and learning. TPR Academy is an English-learning school that caters to children and adults outside of normal school and work hours.

Navid introduced himself and began his lecture. Soon after, I tuned out.

His opening remarks were about the value and importance of education, that the job we had as educators was not only to impart knowledge but to impart wisdom and morals. He talked about a spiritual education. He talked about being a role model, a nurturer—that parents and teachers share this responsibility. I slouched down and thought, "Oh boy, here we go."

You may wonder why, as his statements seem harmless, if not accurate. But I'd heard this sentiment and rhetoric before—under the ownership of groups and administrations back in America whose view of the world runs counter to mine, and their talk of "a need for an education" is often used as leverage for their policy.

I had grown tired of the propaganda.

So when Navid started talking like "one of them," my defenses went up. And so it could have gone for the next two hours, veiled from truth due to my judgments—*just the kind of thing I moved abroad to improve.* Thankfully, I didn't tune out Navid for long. As he spoke of the upcoming classes, it was beginning to sink in that it might not be as easy as I had anticipated. That Saturday I would have fifteen sets of eyes staring back at me. Imagine that—fifteen little Chinese kids looking up at you, or worse, not looking at you because they're bored or messing around with one another. Though I assumed they would be good and quiet, I considered what I'd do if they did get out of line. Then, all the factors to consider when teaching children also hit me: some are louder, some quiet, some smarter, some respond to different learning styles, and some want to be there more than others. And, I would be teaching five different classes—five combinations of all these factors. *Oh, and all the names.* And how long does fifty minutes in the classroom feel anyhow?

Nothing like the reality of reality to get you out of the luxury of being an ideologue.

Adding to all this, I had thought that my job would be to simply, well, teach. Navid used the analogy that the teacher is an urn full of water, and it is their job to fill all the little urns. "All right," I thought. I liked this analogy—clear, simple. Problem was, he used this dated idea to contrast how far we've come in our understanding of education since the ancient Greeks used this very analogy. Hmmm, seems like my prejudices and ignorance had me behind the times just a titch. So I told myself to be quiet and listen, and from an open mind came open eyes, realizing the fulfillment of what was ahead.

Socrates: filling urns

Navid went on to promote another idea of education: that inside each student is a pearl. Some are easy to find, easy to shine. Others are not. Our job as teachers was to discover this pearl inside each child and learn how to make it shine. This is what it is to teach—not merely passing knowledge down, but a discovery process, an interaction that should motivate, educate, and help another person grow. Whoa. Once I heard this, it wasn't just fear of that upcoming Saturday that got me to focus—it was excitement about getting to participate in this process. In addition, I thought of the character and the skills honed as a result of teaching: creativity, patience, expression, focus, and confidence.

Mr. Holland: shining pearls

The Greek illustration was powerful for another reason. It revealed that education is something that's been studied for a long time—well before lobbies and political lawn signs. It revealed to me the importance of this topic. Indeed, what could be more important than how knowledge and wisdom get passed down? How else do we grow as a people?

Education is so much bigger than politics. But I realized how easy it is for me to take a side on an issue and then disregard anything that resembles the opposition. Lesson learned. Breakthroughs may be months/years in the making, but they happen in a moment. On this morning, I realized what a lucky opportunity I had before me. And it was a good thing, too, because I'd need the energy and motivation to get me through the tougher classes and tougher days.

***

Student, Teacher

My first morning of teaching, I awoke early, ready, and anxious for a full day of handing out books and getting to know my students. It was Saturday, which, along with Sundays, were my busiest days of the week with morning 'til night children's classes. During the week we'd have the occasional after-school course, but mainly, weekdays were for our adult evening classes.

I walked to the ordinarily busy bus stop near my apartment, but found it quiet at 8:30 a.m. on a weekend. (I couldn't say the same for on the way home.) After a fifteen-minute ride, I got off the bus, crossed the street to the same town square I offered my Chinese dance debut the week prior, walked into the Ning Xi branch...

...and introduced myself to the friendly receptionist.

Who directed me to my class

I walked in my room at ten minutes to nine, set my bag down, and prepared the materials for my first class. Moments later, they began to arrive—their mom, dad, or grandparent taking them by the hand and guiding them inside the classroom. I pulled up a chair near the whiteboard at the front the room. Most were shy as I had each one come over to me. I said hello, shook their little hands, and then, if they had an English name, had them write it on the white board. Those that did held the marker like a pencil in their adorable little hands, curling their t's, j's and i's just like their primary school teachers had taught them. They were my youngest students—six-year-olds, eighteen of them.

Class picture taken later in the term

With all the students present and in their desks arranged in a U-shaped row along the rear and side walls of the classroom, I stood and said "good morning" and "welcome to TPR." They just looked back at me. My teaching assistant then stood from her desk to do her part. (TPR, like typical English learning centers in China, has bi-lingual teaching assistants—TAs—who sit in the classrooms to interpret for beginner students. Typically, TAs were women in their early twenties.) With her help, I gave the children my name and then segued into what I thought would be a fun activity for them: getting to choose their own English names for those without. One veteran teacher had told me beforehand to simply assign them a name and get on with it. But I thought, "Pshaw to that. I'm not their dad. These kids should have the chance to come up with their own identity."

I brought the first student up, leaned down, and asked them what they'd like their name to be. The child just stared straight ahead. "All right," I thought. "This can be a good way to get the other kids involved." So I stood up and asked the class to come up with some names.

Silence.

Such a task proved difficult as the young pupils didn't seem to know any. Okay, how about I let the student choose from a list I come up with? On the whiteboard I wrote: Jennifer, Charles, Gordon, Angela, Rebecca, Susan, Aaron, Carl, John, etc. Names are practically endless, but my mind got stuck at about twenty. Even so, some students wanted more options. So I finally did for some what the veteran teacher more or less recommended all along and steered them toward a couple to pick from: "Do you want Amanda or Cynthia?"

After naming, I had them all come up to the front of the class where a map of the world hung.

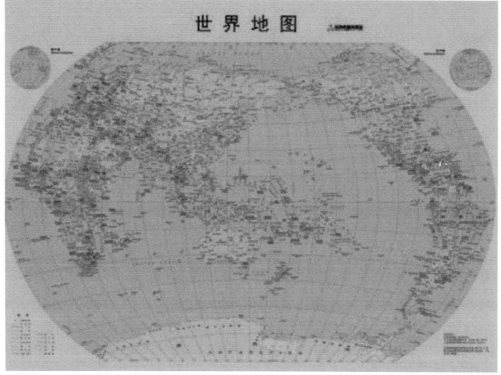

I pointed out Minnesota, and motioned an arc mimicking the flight I had taken just two weeks prior.

With introductions over, the students sat back down while I paused for the acknowledgement that it was now time to teach. As I began to gather the workbooks to distribute, I looked up to realize these shy children were no longer so. I guess while I was introducing myself, they were getting to know one another. They had no problem filling my pause with their own activity. I walked up to a couple chatting with each other. "Shh," I said while giving them a somewhat stern look. They quieted, but doing this turned my back to those on the opposite side of the room. These kids then started to chat. Turning around and walking up to them then created the same issue with two new students. I was losing the proverbial game of whack-a-mole—they were now a collective with a will of their own and a propensity to break apart into trios or pairs if need be to keep the chaos alive. I had to settle them down—darn near impossible. (Well, impossible for Mr. Rookie Teacher here.)

It wasn't just talk either—now they were moving about. When in the midst of all that, what do you do—yell? A father of one of my students told me in those early days that I had to be tougher. He feared his quiet daughter was getting a little snuffed out in all the rowdiness. She was. Thankfully, for these youngest ones classes were just fifty minutes long. So before too long, and after the TA and I did our best to manage the chatter, time was up. But I was left wondering what happened to the soldier students. Subsequent classes were twice as long, but the students were older. As a general rule I would find that the older, the easier.

Another problem that first weekend was that *I* was undisciplined. When teaching, I shrugged off much of that annoying weight called responsibility and didn't pay too much attention to the fact that I had a job to do. "Lesson plans? We'll get to that later," I thought. I taught whatever came to mind—this noun, that verb. Imagine the carefree ease with which you could walk into a strange school, teach for a day, and then leave. No worries about tests or parents. That's how I saw that first weekend. I had been so carefree, in fact, that I took my TA by surprise. She apparently contacted Navid, who then called me on Monday to ask if I had been drinking before class. Initially insulted, I can now look back and realize that there may have been better ways to try to teach the word "throw" than by picking up a chair and pretending to toss it.

This was how my teaching career started.

There was a lot of learning going on those first days. Unfortunately, I was the one being educated about all that I didn't know regarding teaching principles and practice.

Chapter Four: Groovin'

With job and routine, I began to settle into the rhythm of life in Zhuhai.

During teacher training Navid gave us a handout on the four stages of living abroad: *Honeymoon*—it's all good; *Hostility*—this place stinks with all its corruption and pollution and no English-language TV; *Humor*—settling in allows you to laugh at yourself and the things around you; and *Home*—in the rhythm of being a regular.

The first stage is the same as what you feel when you travel—at least when I do. Problems and inconveniences can seem quaint, even comical: a cot with one-inch mattress to sleep on, a terribly narrow and curvy mountain road on which our bus passes semi-trailers while making a corner, being cautioned to put away my camera from opportunistic thieves, no hot water, and so on. These were just the circumstances in which I found myself in foreign lands I visited. They were what they were and nothing more. Freshness and impermanence; objectivity and disconnectedness prevented agitation from sticking and setting in, and allow for a glass-is-half-full perspective. It wasn't the low quality of the bike that occurred to me, it was that Marilyn and I had a tandem bike to use at all.

Back home in Minneapolis, though, never mind a bike—I was embarrassed by the car I drove because it was old and noisy. And potholes I hit occasionally made me angry at the city. Because now it was *my* lousy car, *my* city's potholes. China, for better and for worse, would become more and more like home. The honeymoon evaporated like a lake revealing its rugged bottom. After just a couple weeks, I grew tired of the idiosyncrasies here. The traffic got old; the fish smells bothered me. I felt rejected if the locals found me invisible and didn't reciprocate my hellos or my smiles. Yet I became annoyed at my obviousness and the way people stared at me because I was different. I guess this was Stage Two.

Causing this, I realized, was my surprisingly strong and automatic tendency to stop noticing my environment—the buildings, that one stray dog, the street salespeople. I drifted toward a more inward focus, and in missing out on the here and now, I became less confident of each step I took and of each interaction I had. I felt restricted, which opposed the extraordinary amount of personal freedom travel usually allowed. But this wasn't typical travel; I was here to live.

I wrote about these feelings one afternoon. By doing so and seeing them in print, it became evident that they came from a skewed reality. Things weren't bad at all; now I just had to let my emotions realize this truth. Like having the flu and acknowledging my grumpiness and negativity because of it, I understood that this bout of anxiety and frustration, though very real, was also only a temporary feeling to see through and let go of. This breakthrough disarmed it, and I saw that nothing was as bad as those feelings implied. I felt relief almost immediately. And then, the obvious was assumed once more: that one has a lot to experience living abroad—and one has a lot to offer others.

I also reached out to friends back home and shared how I felt. And in addition to corresponding with them, one actually knew an American attorney named George living just a few miles away from me in Macau. And upon emailing him, he put me in touch with his friend living in Zhuhai, a retired Australian expat named Paul. Paul and I would soon start meeting over coffee and building a friendship. I was impressed all year by the impact even one face-to-face, heart-to-heart connection can have. Not only did it compel me out of my negativity, but it helped guide me toward making China feel like home.

From the vantage point these actions put me on, I learned that the key to an enjoyable, active year would be in trying to recapture/retain the freshness of a new land—the presence to fully be wherever I was, to notice all about me, to maintain my traveling mentality while settling in. It's a tough line to walk; we tend to have distinct mindsets for travel and home. China would be a blend. Would the language and social differences be a constant novelty or an annoyance—a help or a burden—in me attaining the fourth stage of feeling at home?

Yes.

***

The Routine Life

China was fresh, exciting, and hour-by-hour, but I also had a work contract, a lease, my bank, my gym, the usual grocery spots—all that "regular" stuff requiring (or at least encouraging) a long-term, hunker-down mentality.

Immediately after I arrived in China, I noticed exercise equipment built within a broad stretch of sidewalk across the street from my complex. These contraptions had to handle the elements, so they were made of solid metal parts that swung and rotated according to the routine they were built for. One was a "steering wheel" that you rotated. Another you stepped upon and rocked your legs opposite of each other back and forth. They were brightly colored and mostly used by older people. Sometimes I'd see children playing on them. I photographed a group of women on one occasion.

Looks like they needed a Chinese Richard Simmons to pop out and get some life into their routine.

Then again, maybe they were just concentrating.

"I WILL get into that size 2!"

I found my own fitness groove at a gym on the fifth floor of the department store, Jusco. (That place had everything.) Off the elevator and down the hallway, I'd enter through the double glass doors where the receptionist counter stood to the left. There, two young women dressed in black pants and black, red-edged blouses held my membership card in exchange for a locker key. After saying "xiè xie" to them, I'd walk past the human-sized plant and wall waterfall; its light, trickling sound centered me toward a smooth, peaceful workout.

Out the lobby was the gym floor—cardio machines to the right, free weights to the left, and weight machines in between. Along the right side of the spacious workout area was the dance/yoga room behind glass windows and door; on the left side was the hot yoga room. Further back were the locker rooms. And here is where idiosyncratic China said hello.

Can you see that down there?

I actually got a kick out of the guys smoking in the locker room. It symbolized that laid-back, guard-let-down policy. "Relax. You're in China," they said to me by puffing away half-naked. Just wear your sandals, a fellow forty-year-old English teacher from Canada would tell me, following this up with his story about getting a foot fungus.

Sometimes for exercise I'd jog the lovely coast. Running along the well-built paths of my choice—stone walking path, asphalt bike path, or grass—the ocean to my right and palm trees to my left energized my legs. Too bad I had to make it through a patch of stench as sewage into the ocean aromatized my cardio.

Often after working out at the gym I'd go grocery shopping a few floors below. Jusco's grocery was modern, clean, and their products were orderly and arranged in aisles familiar with any large US grocer. Most products were Chinese-inspired—either by cuisine and/or company.

This is clearly an amazing product.

But it also offered some welcomed Western goods such as dairy products (cheese was hard to find in China). And even more direct from America, were these recognizable foods and brands:

These product shots are courtesy of Edward Robert Blevins at thekunmingreport.com. Check out his blog for current goings-on in one of the most interesting provinces in China, Yunnan.

Like the gym, Jusco's grocery also had its China "charm." The meat aisle stood out with fish smell, alligator chilled on ice, and this specimen hung for all to hunger after:

Imagine this in the middle of the floor at your store. Conveniently, it was just an aisle or two down from the cleaning supplies.

Produce was expensive, so I usually took to the outdoor fruit vendors for my apples and bananas. Many of these roller-grocers would cart around their portable stores. Others would have small, stationary outdoor operations. It was like the sweet corn or pumpkin stands along rural Minnesotan roads in the fall. But unlike the Minnesotan pumpkin peddler, these urban operations were less earthy and more grimy. Buyer beware. I once bit into an apple to find a black pit inside. From then on, I looked closely at them. One plus about these operations were the oddly late hours they kept.

Alley near my apartment at 11:00 p.m.

I ate peanut butter sandwiches or oatmeal for most breakfasts. For lunch or dinner, I would often prepare ramen noodle soup and add premade frozen dumplings. At least once a week I ate sushi from the inexpensive mom-and-pop sushi counters in my neighborhood. Stored at air temperature for unknown lengths of time, I wondered if it was safe to eat, but I never got sick from it. I'd also frequently visit a small husband and wife-owned restaurant a block from my home. They had great dumplings and good beef noodle soup. They got to know me and knew what I wanted before I said anything. Three yuan for six dumplings and five for the soup. A total of eight yuan meant a meal for about $1.30.

In one alley near my apartment, there were eight small eateries side-by-side. Though all sold Chinese food, there was still quite a variety: dumplings, soup, rice dishes, noodles, and plenty of meat and vegetarian options.

Handwritten menus on the wall showed the options. If lucky, there would also be pictures to go by.

Away from the alleys and stalls were larger, independent dine-in restaurants ranging from a cement floor room with cafeteria seating and florescent lighting to those with shiny wood floors, plush leather booths, and a grand piano in the corner. The prices ranged from twelve yuan all the way up to eighty in a couple places I went. But for an average dine-in meal, you're looking at twenty-five to thirty yuan. No tipping in China.

Often when sitting down at a restaurant in Zhuhai, one finds a white glass bowl, saucer, cup, and spoon all stacked together and shrink-wrapped. The custom is to pop the plastic wrap with a chopstick, tear it off, and then use the hot tea provided to wash the ware.

At this restaurant, a worker did the honors.

I always found this routine curious considering the other examples where sanitation lagged.

The above restaurant's toilet

This bathroom was typical. And that garbage bin at eleven o'clock? That was for used toilet paper because these things like to plug up. Also, you need to remember to have your own toilet paper. Just like napkins at the restaurant, it is rarely provided. I would later have a semi-scary incident going from stall to stall seeking some tissue. BYOTP.

In the fast food world, KFC is king in China, outdoing McDonald's in market share 2:1. Regardless, there are a couple of each to be had in Zhuhai. We also had a Papa John's and two Starbucks. Starbucks was admittedly nice—not only for the coffee-drinker (restaurants typically had only instant coffee, if any at all), but because the cozy confines of carpet, temperature control, and a leather chair was a far cry from the small, plastic stools and tiled floors baking in the summer and cold in the winter. Fast food franchises looked similar to those in America, but menus could be adjusted. KFC had rice soup as well and hot soy milk which I found surprisingly delicious for breakfast in the winter. I also found these restaurants quite expensive. And when I say expensive, I mean similarly-priced as they are back home, but on a Chinese wage, $5 (32RMB) isn't insignificant. However, despite costing more than double for what you could get a good meal elsewhere, these Western joints were reliably busy.

At night, one back street in my neighborhood turned into a nightly outdoor food festival. This popular late-night dining experience is known in China simply as "Barbeque"; I saw it in several cities all over the country. Propane-powered, rectangular grills cooked the food of your choice—and it was quite a choice. Large tables with fresh vegetables, meats on sticks, and seafood options spread before you. You grabbed a plastic basket, placed your edibles inside, told them what you wanted to drink, and found a place at one of many collapsible, four-person tables surrounded by plastic outdoor chairs. At this particular location, there were several of these operations competing and working together to create this festive, beer-drinking, cigarette-smoking social for locals—and sometimes for foreigners, too.

Cheers. Heath and other teachers enjoying a Barbeque dinner.

***

Getting Around

Walking was the most common mode of transportation for me. The fluidity between pedestrian and car in Chinese cities created quite an intimate dance. I can't count the number of times I could've reached out to pet the cars as they swooped by in front of me, eager to make that left turn at an intersection. Pedestrians are just as direct. If not for metal pipe-fence dividers screwed down between opposite lanes on busy roads, people would run across. Some still jumped the dividers to prevent a longer walk to the nearest crosswalk or pedestrian underpass. (I did this myself when in a pinch heading to school. When in Rome.)

I didn't see one car pulled over by police all year. I was told freeways had cameras, though. This is all a bit moot, however, because out-of-country folk cannot drive unless they pass the Chinese driving exam. In my year, I encountered just one foreigner who had a Chinese driver's license. He was Reynold, the fellow new American (Oregonian) teacher a couple years younger than I with a medium build, glasses, and a warm, reserved nature. His Chinese was so good, in fact, that he opted to take the test in Mandarin despite the option to take it in English. For most all visitors to Zhuhai, though, it's foot, bus, and taxi (or tandem bicycle).

Zhuhai taxis are a fleet of Volkswagons

Zhuhai city bus

The buses in the city, when need be, filled themselves to levels never before thought possible. They weren't any larger than city buses I've seen all over the world, yet they could and would hold ninety people. I counted.

Some of these longer bus trips were arduous when standing. All the way, you vibrate and jerk and lean on the rattling ride. The fear of being fated to such a tiring trial caused crowds to run alongside the bus as it slows to its stop with the hopes of getting on first. I didn't want any part of that dangerous theater; however, I did once dart from the curb to our bus's door with all the urgency I believed necessary to get a seat on a lengthy ride out of town. Little did I know that on this route both the front and back (typically the exit) doors opened for new riders, and when they did so I could only look on as two swarms filled the seats. I really hurried at that point, but Chinese butts were in place moments before I could get my derriere there, and so mine was without a seat and my feet took the brunt of the load.

Once, when demonstrated before us, Eva, my school's teacher relations employee, felt compelled to defend to me her people's eagerness to board a bus or, as I saw at a potluck, to "line up" for food as if they hadn't any back home. She explained this as a learned trait stemming from the scarcity of the 1950s and 60s. Back then, the famine-inducing government programs, The Great Leap Forward and the Cultural Revolution, took place. Perhaps Eva was right. Regardless, I didn't look down my nose. It's not as if Americans don't overreact for Black Friday or even when a fast food restaurant gives away a free coffee.

I do need to say that during the non-rush hour ride, the back of the bus—which sits up a little taller to make way for the engine beneath—provided a enjoyable vantage point from which to view the city or read a book. Bus travel also provided a big benefit: meeting people. I can recall many times preparing for the class I was heading toward and having my materials trigger a conversation with my bus seat neighbor—whether young, old, man, or woman. We'd talk about why I was in Zhuhai, and in turn, why they were, happily speaking what little English and what little Chinese each other knew.

***

After laying the groundwork for getting around and getting by, things in China were kicked up a notch. If I got my feet wet before, now I dove right in.

PART 2: Lessons and Themes

Chapter 5: A Relationship With China

A growing intimacy with life here nurtured some powerful lessons learned.

Feminine Power

I did yoga at my gym. Why not? It's part of the membership fee. Plus, I really liked the meditative benefits of doing so. It also made me sweat a lot, and I assume that to be a good thing. One time when I arrived, though, lingual confusion had me take part in something much less likely for a man to try.

I came to class this weekday afternoon ready to stretch and pose. After changing into my blue gym shorts and black tee shirt, I walked into the yoga room, grabbed a blue yoga mat, took off my shoes and socks, and started to stretch. I picked a spot in the center of the room surrounded by mainly middle-aged women. By now I had gotten used to usually being the only non-Chinese and only male. But soon one stout, short-haired woman whom I'd met before and who knew a bit of English greeted me in such a way as to reveal some surprise at me being there. I gave another look around and wondered.

Then the instructor arrived—a young, athletic woman dressed in white tank top and maroon sweatpants. When I asked about the class, she conveyed through my acquaintance that this was "balance class." Oh, okay. Well, it's not yoga, but whatever. Balance sounds cool. So I decided to stay put. Our instructor walked to the front and put a CD in the stereo along the right wall. She pressed "play," walked to front center, and stood facing her class of twenty-five evenly-spaced students.

The music began. She began. I raised my eyebrows in surprise.

After the first beat of the first song, I knew this was far beyond the gender-neutral territory of yoga. The music was slow, light, and passionate. The instructor's lead wasn't poses but smooth and methodic dance moves: light touches, limp wrists, and weightless limbs. I feebly followed her lead along with the others. I was self-conscious, but something about being away from home allowed me the freedom to not care so much. My thin frame moved awkwardly—particularly compared to the instructor, even compared to the stout middle-agers—but I gave it my light-footed, light-hearted best. And after just a minute of letting myself go to the art, I felt something in my hands and arms and then in my whole body. Whatever that something was, the dance leader exuded it.

One move was a lifting of the hands—wrists touching—raising in front of the chest, then face, then the sky as wrists parted. It let you feel the air like your limbs were moving through water.

Only there was no water. The substance explored—as odd as this sounds—was life. Doing the routine, I became acutely aware of my life, of life in general.

I had actually been introduced to the term *feminine power* in the months prior and couldn't help but recall those words right here and now. It seemed I had a definition for it offered by the feelings resulting from this bodily expression. I felt the power of growth, potential, hope—and most of all—an appreciation, love, and dedication to life, to living. This opposed the only aspects of power I had known: domination, competition, proving yourself, demonstrating your worth by defeating or conquering something—an opponent, a barbell, a goal, a calculus problem, a trophy buck, a competing business, another country. There was still some element of "fight" in this "feminine" form of power, but even this felt to be a passionate battle that moves delicately—not physically aggressive, but patient, persisting, nurturing, and soaking in every moment. How beautiful, how important, how...powerful!

From the start, China had provided a new way of expressing femininity and masculinity.

Pictures of male trainers from my gym

Zhuhai's residents embodied an interpersonal closeness:

Probably not lesbians

Probably not gay

In China—at least southern China—many men carried themselves with a more delicate walk, prettied hair, and some sported lengthy, manicured fingernails. Fisherman and other figures of masculinity commonly pulled their shirts up over their midriffs.

Young men out for a evening in Zhuhai

By being here, and by participating in this (and subsequent) "balance" classes, I gained an appreciation of *feminine power*—and *masculine power* by way of comparison. I also realized the societal value and embodiment along this continuum of femininity/masculinity. It seems its expression influences national aspects of business, art, policy, and philosophy. Specifically, I thought about how China conducts foreign policy, and then I thought about the US approach; I thought about US domestic policy and how popular it is to address a social ailment by having a "war" with it.

It occurred to me just how far-tilted America is toward the masculine, so much so that femininity and gender equality are measured in masculine terms.

I came to believe that an unfortunate result of this bias is twofold: it limited my own exposure and appreciation for *feminine power* (if not for an accident, I wouldn't have taken part in this class), and it prevents the power I experienced in class from being celebrated and shared on a societal plane. I learned that gender appreciation and equality are not about pretending the differences between the masculine and feminine aren't there. It's about realizing that the traits of femininity are not inferior. I also learned that masculinity and femininity aren't synonymous with male and female.

Overall, by missing out on the powerful beauty displayed in this class, I believe we restrict our potential on the continuum of the human experience.

***

Western Men, Chinese Women

My colleague Steve was an Australian in his fifties. He was six feet tall, thinly built with a bit of a gut, wore glasses, and had graying hair and a peppered beard that he said he grew to divert attention from his jutting nose and chin. Steve knew lots of things and had been to lots of places and liked to talk. He had been in Zhuhai teaching English for about nine years.

While we walked along the sidewalks of Zhuhai one afternoon, Steve opened up to me about the sexual aspects of moving to China. He first let me in on his version of events that ended his marriage back in Australia years before. His divorce put the kibosh on a successful banana farming operation, gutted his finances, and ended with alienation from his kids. To him, the differences between Eastern and Western women were as obvious as his preference.

"I don't like Western women," he said to me as we walked. "They are bullying and treat you like dog shit. I don't like being treated like dog shit." Steve's Chinese girlfriend(s) on the other hand, "look after the house, look after you. They're kind and polite," he said.

Days later, I met for coffee with Paul, the retired Australian expat whom I was put in touch with when I reached out to friends back home. Paul was nearing sixty, a bit overweight, and had a weathered face. It was on our second visit that he opened up about his relationships. Unlike Steve, Paul gets along fine with his Australian ex, but like Steve, differentiates the styles of how Chinese women treat their men.

"They treat you like a king," he said to me. Paul was married to a Chinese woman twenty-five years younger and added, "I haven't shaved in a year." He then offered wincing examples of other hygienic duties some women here, including his wife, assume—clipping his toenails and popping his blackheads.

[Later in the year, I did catch a young woman doing this to her boyfriend in public. I assume this to be traditional behavior, as I'm doubtful I'd see this from women trying to be more modern.]

Their women seemed to provide comforts Paul and Steve longed for. Feeling that his ex took him to the cleaners made a hot breakfast and a shave feel like heaven to Steve I'm sure. Paul was equally willing to enjoy these benefits as he came to China falling on very hard times. He was severely depressed, so a friend from back home took him for a "night out on the town" in Macau. Having such a good time with the Macanese prostitutes, Paul decided to extend his stay— eighteen months and counting as we sat over coffee.

Being servile was just part of the sphere of feminine behavior, though. Both Steve and Paul also shared instances of women being very forward. Steve told me soon after about a woman in business attire rubbing herself against him on the bus. I thought she might have been trying to rub-rob him. Not the case, he insisted. Over another coffee a week or two later, Paul then told me of a woman on the bus sending her foot up his leg while they were both seated. Going on about the uniqueness of these women, he exclaimed, "They'll put their foot in your nuts!"

He was also holding her phone number soberly in his hands while telling me this. He wasn't sure what to do with it. He was now married, and his wife carried his only child.

"They're ruthless," he said looking at the number. "They'll steal you from your gal."

Not dealing with the drama of divorce or children, the younger Western guys in Zhuhai fraternized in lighter fare. Soon after I arrived, a light-complexioned, twenty-five-year-old American English teacher offered this gem, said with a cheesy grin, "You ever heard of the 'times ten' rule?"

"No", I responded.

"Well, it's that however hot you were in your home country, you're ten times that here."

[There are plenty of ideas floating around as to why Chinese women like Western guys. I wondered if there would be an ongoing issue of local men getting angry when "their" women favored foreigners, but the trend wasn't seen by me.]

Heath had himself a Chinese girlfriend. She was sweet and polite and pretty; she was perhaps twenty-three-years-old, dressed casually, and liked to go shopping with friends. Heath had been her teacher. Her English was basic, however, and his Mandarin negligible; I wondered what they talked about.

I was twenty-nine and single. I felt stuck in the polarity of cross-culture dating. While there were lots of women around (one could see them all), there were no women around (one couldn't talk to hardly any of them). That didn't stop a lot of the other guys. One night I was watching TV at one of the two Western bars in town when a thirty-year-old red-headed Englishman named Thom called me over to sit with him and a friend. I had met these two a couple nights before and took them to be two of the more socially-connected guys in town. I asked them about their dating lives, whether they found it difficult to connect with local women. Thom's friends swung his head back in laughter at the notion. I wasn't sure whether he did so because he had no problem meeting women or because he had no interest in starting a relationship.

He simply said, "Don't ever tell them that you love them. They get too attached."

My summation was that while it seemed easy to get a girlfriend in China, it also seemed harder to find a romantic interest. I didn't think I'd find a partner due to the lingual and cultural bridges. The schism was just too wide for hearts to cross. And the examples of cross-cultural dating and relationships around me only added to that belief.

***

What Teaching is Teaching Me

By mid-fall, my most consistent activity bore fruit as a catalyst for many lessons, some of which weren't about education at all.

Adulthood

My fantastical approach of ignoring lesson plans quickly evaporated as I was reminded by colleagues that students had to pass a test at semester's end—and my classes had fallen behind. Convinced I had to focus, I now had to persuade some of my tougher students to do the same. Some teachers told me to involve such kids who were really acting up. I tried that with one problematic, chubby six-year-old boy who would always slam his desk, squirm in his seat, and when I told him to be quiet would just give me a toothy, showy grin. He'd run up to the white board when I wasn't looking and steal a marker. He insisted on sitting next to the door and playing with the lock or open the door at random times during class. I tried to have him sit away from the door, but he hated that. And because he was big, getting him to move required his full participation. Thankfully, his mom saw him from the lobby one day as he opened the door in class. She barged in, grabbed him by the arm, and scolded him with her finger in his face. That got him to straighten up—for several minutes anyway. Oh, and the experiment of getting him more involved didn't work the way I wanted either. As my "white board writing assistant" he just took the liberty to draw what he wanted. He stood out, but he wasn't the only one whom I had trouble teaching.

One weekday in mid-October a teaching mentor monitored my class as I taught a group of fifteen after-school six-year-olds. During an evidently not-too-riveting lesson, my mentor stood up during a lull and approached to ask if he could take over. This middle-aged, short and stout gentleman named Riaz—like Navid, he was also Persian—then stood in front of my class, hunched toward the students sitting in their desks, and got all big-eyed and open-mouthed. "Hey class!" he said excitedly. Then he swiftly showed them a laminated picture of a cartoon cat. "What's this?!" Those students—who by this time had been bored to death—perked right up and started answering his questions. I couldn't believe it. Literally three minutes earlier some had their faces in their hands with eyes barely open.

I had been hesitant to speak to my young classes like they were, well, children. I thought the exaggerated expressions one gives to babies would be demeaning for those old enough to walk and talk. But I discovered that children's high energy and short attention spans, indeed, need to be met with high energy, and quick, little lessons. (Seems pretty obvious now.) It turned out my reaction to falling behind with my classes—that it was time to seriously "get down to business"— also missed the mark.

So I went to Jusco and found some hand puppets of cute, little animals. The white board on wheels in our class allowed me to stand behind and puppeteer an English lesson atop.

My nine-year-olds named them Cookie, Cake, and Ice Cream.

I would teach our lesson's adjectives by acting them out. A tall, cane-handled umbrella left behind in my apartment from a previous teacher made for a nice prop when wobbling around the room to describe "old."

Drawings helped, too.

By eventually learning to have fun with the students while following the lesson plan, I began to discover the art of being carefree without being careless. In other words—be an adult and do my job: handle the concerns of naughty kids and involved parents, maintain my own desire to see the students learn, and keep things light. I began to blossom into a real teacher here in China. If this were a movie, I'd offer you a montage with a song like "Everybody's Working for the Weekend" (though most of my teaching *was* on the weekend). The music plays with cut scenes showing me in my apartment preparing lesson plans, giving puppet shows to my younger classes behind the white board, talking with parents, teaching with big eyes and wide mouth to my young children, speaking like an adult—though slowly—to my adults, and finally, a shot of me getting off the bus walking home in my neighborhood of old downtown Zhuhai as the scene fades into black.

Though I sometimes wished I wasn't so tied down in order to be freer to travel about, it was this working life that provided meaning and self-worth. It also allowed me to be on the same level as the people I was amongst—just another cog in the system, helping me to know what it was truly like living here day in, day out. My job also helped me get to know my students.

Childhood

Unburdened of work, money, and status, my wee ones' freedom to be silly and expressive week after week was eye-opening.

In the minutes before class, my group of nine-year-olds (including the boy above) mingled with enthusiasm. Boys played whatever game was trendy—a card game of cartoon zombies and killer plants comes to mind. The girls tended to exercise the bonds of friendship by chatting giddily in groups or pairing up to talk in secret—perhaps a beginning acknowledgement that information is precious and ought not be for all to hear, or perhaps the germination of the seeds of embarrassment for being expressive and genuine in front others. To be sure, a few kids would just chill by themselves, but despite such introversion or embarrassment, a youthful exhibition of social excitement marked my child students.

Their actions caused me to reflect on a day when I was ten years old and sitting at my desk in class approaching the day's end. Once the dismissal bell sounded, a group of us boys shot up out of our desks and huddled over by the coat rack glowing with the energy of each other's company, anticipating a friend's birthday sleepover. This energy kept us up all night if parents let it. This same social excitement lasted up through my early teen years when a couple buddies and I would stay up all night talking in a tent in each other's backyards. (How many of us, as adults, can get such a thrill to stay up all night just by talking with friends?) Well, I had grown-up students, too, serving as a nice comparison to my excitable youngsters; minutes prior to their class they'd also converse but in a monotone "Hey man, how you doing?" kind of way.

To be fair, my young students had another beneficial trait adding to their enjoyment: imagination and make-believe.

The distance of 7,700 miles between Minneapolis and Zhuhai didn't change the fact that boys love playing "guns." I liked to join in with these nine-year-olds before we began our lesson, but I was severely outmatched. Turns out that a bigger factor trumped distance or culture in our play compatibility: age.

I came armed with a pointer-finger pistol. These boys were tossing grenades equipped with some sort of audible digital timer that they detonated from their wrists. Then they shot me with weapons which take five seconds just to pantomime prepare. All the loading, and pumping, and assembling, and cocking of their bells-and-whistles modern-day weaponry allowed me 14 bangs to their one BOOOOOUUSHHHHHSHSHSHSHH!!! Too bad my pea-shooter wasn't even audible over their awesome weapon warm-up.

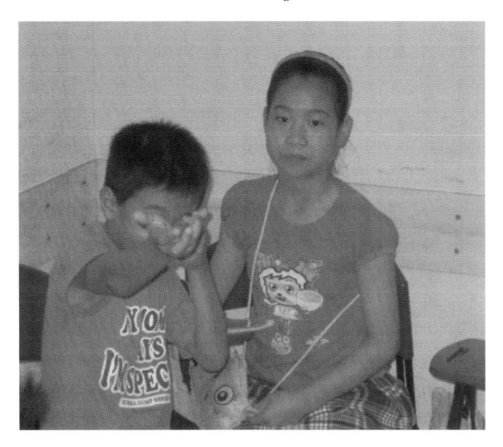

That being said, I did play a nice monster, impenetrable to their sophisticated arsenal. Slowly walking toward them with my arms held straight out, to them I was that monster and to a magically perfect degree—real enough to get them excited, but not too real to seriously freak them out.

I observed them run around like it was the first time I ever saw children playing. Growing up with younger siblings and cousins, this activity was something I just took for granted, but here in the freshness of a foreign land I saw just how cool it is that kids' minds allow for this excitement. My Chinese students inspired me to pay closer attention forthwith. After returning home, I watched my nephew play with a toy man on a motorcycle on his living room floor. He added sound effects. "Vrrrrrrrrr" it raced along the carpet toward the ramp; "vooooooo" it glided through the air; "pshh!" it landed safely on the other side of the obstacle. The adults in the room passively watched the scene, probably thinking, "Kids just playing." I thought about what was going on inside my nephew's head. He is that motorcycle man living out the amazing.

A child's world can magically take on this other reality, one that has them live out the dreams of stardom, superhero-dom, defeating monsters, or playing house. It seems to be their mental rehearsal for all that they are capable of accomplishing in adulthood when that blurred sense of reality dissipates. Then responsibilities are added, challenging one's ability to reach as far as their imaginations once took them. And as I learned above, fantasy can even be a liability in adulthood—me ignoring those lesson plans. But the payoff is that in adulthood you're given the chance to live out these dreams not just in fantasy, but in actuality.

Conversely, I wonder if my nephew watches us adults and thinks, "How can they just sit there and talk? Or watch that boring TV show of those people just talking?" It's much more enjoyable to play, as my students demonstrated in various classes of mine.

Moving up in age, it was striking to see the change that takes place in young people in just a few years. I didn't teach many teenagers, but if the one class of fourteen- to fifteen-year-olds I did teach was any indication, then it seems that either preteen energy lessens or redistributes, fearlessness wears off, or a garment of fear or social order gets added. Perhaps it's a combination thereof.

These students were quiet, slightly uncomfortable, and reluctant to come to the front of the class for a demonstration when asked. An eight-year-old might decide to hop like a bunny if asked to come forward. Conversely, one fourteen-year-old young man slowly shuffled up to the front with slumped shoulders as if thinking, "Why me?"

[A terrific example of this is played out in the classic British documentary, Seven Up. *In it, fourteen seven-year-olds are interviewed. They are then revisited and interviewed every seven years. In 2012, "56 Up" was released. Of all the episodes (most of which are available on YouTube), the most drastic change occurs from age seven to fourteen. Almost all the children go from smiling, spry youths to serious, quiet, and shy adolescents.]*

Brotherhood

Of all the Chinese people with whom I interacted during my year, my adult students produced some of my most meaningful connections. My first such class were peers by age and by life situation, an even mixture of men and women early in their careers. I first arrived to this class eager to be able to teach a group I wouldn't have to constantly monitor. Class was held down in the Gongbei branch, a fourth-floor cozy, carpeted office space in a nice hotel.

Each adult class had around ten students sitting in a semicircle. They already had English names, so I started things off by going to the map and showing them where I was from. I continued to break the ice by sharing about Minnesota winters. As I told them about chipping ice and snow off our windshields, some spurted surprise laughter. They let out even more when hearing about driving cars onto the lake to go fishing. (Fast forward to later in the year, and they were shocked when I shared that my grandfather owned twenty guns. I tried to bridge this gap and ask them in a few different ways about China's no-gun policy, always looking for an exception: "What about rural China?" or "What about for hunting?" or "What if you have livestock and a wolf is eating them?" They replied "Nope" to all three. Guns were never in the hands of civilians.)

They were intermediate English language learners, which meant they both knew and didn't know a lot. We held three two-hour classes per week opening each with conversation ("What did you do over the weekend?") Then we would review the grammar lesson, listen to a cheesy conversation on CD, do a writing exercise, and have the students practice speaking, reading, and so on.

Judy, a student and employee of the school; and, Jackie, a government employee

My friend, Jerry, and Rebecca

I preferred this setting. Classes always went smoothly as long as I planned enough effective activities.

I admired their hard work to further themselves—many of them investing their own money for these classes. It was also great learning about their lives and about China through classroom conversation. Most impactful, though, was the extension of outside-the-class interactivity. Emily, an accountant, took the same bus home as I did and taught me a few Chinese phrases, as well as shared her love of hiking the hills around Zhuhai—sometimes alone and sometimes with her husband.

Jerry, a hotel worker, would be a dear friend to me my whole time in China. When we'd hang out outside of class, he would candidly answer my questions. "One China," he responded when I asked about Taiwan, the island off China's coast that claims national sovereignty. China claims ownership, and Jerry defended that stance by adding, "Taiwan is like a bad son that needs to be punished." He, too, would teach me some Mandarin and went a little further to reel me in if crossing the norms; one time he cautioned me as I spoke too loudly at a restaurant. While he expanded my knowledge, I stretched his boundaries—once when I said hello to an armed guard standing at attention by the gate of a government building. The guard just smiled back and Jerry and I talked to the young man about his job. Jerry and I also would talk about women and relationships as easily as my friends and I would back in America. I'd call his phone out of the blue when in a lingual pinch, and he'd always gladly help translate. Everyone needs a Jerry when traveling abroad!

At the end of the term (adults had quarter terms, children had semesters), adult students traditionally took their teacher out to celebrate. Concluding my time with this class in late October, we went out in classic style around these parts: dinner and karaoke.

On our way to dinner

Jackie, the government employee, drove us to the large, two-story restaurant. He and I dropped the girls off at the door and found a tight spot in the lot of the Sichuan eatery. It was a big place with the main dining hall greeting you upon entry and two more upper floors with smaller dining areas. After walking up a couple flights, Jackie and I approached the gang.

Sichuan is a province in west-central China where the cuisine is legendarily spicy. But despite my students being residents of not-so-spicy Guangdong province, they had no qualms with eating this food. Nor did they think twice about ordering it despite me and my mundane Midwest palate's protestations. Consequently, I had to be careful. And thankfully, I was such a good English teacher they could tell me which dishes to avoid.

It's common to be served "family style" at restaurants all over China. Looking at all the voluminous dishes, you think there'll be ample leftovers, but I constantly surprised myself by how much I could eat—a nibble here and there and a way of always having room for "one more."

I did try one spicy plate, and after just a small bite could sense a tingle grow into a burn. All I could do was sit, wait, and wonder how my tablemates ate mouthfuls as casually as if it were a bowl of white rice. My students noticed my reaction and then pointed to another dish, warning me to stay away from it—because that one was *really* hot.

Afterwards, we went to the karaoke bar. In these places, groups gathered in individual rooms where plush couches lined the walls in a dimly lit space with a table in the center for games, food, and drink. You'll also find microphones, a tambourine, and of course, a big screen television with cheesy videos to go along with the song and lyrics. Beer and snacks were served, but it didn't take any liquid courage to get this show on the road. All my students found it agreeable to sing—no matter how well or poorly they did so. They were remarkably less self-conscious than my American friends.

Croon, Jerry, croon.

Wail, Jackie, wail.

And on we performed 'til a late hour prompted us to our homes. They were an awesome class.

Through them, as well as others I would come to build relationships with, China wasn't just a novel place I found myself in but became a place I built a life around—an urban home like any other where most the folks around you are strangers, yet you feel the belonging and connectedness via the appendages of friendship with others within the city. And when I hung out with my Chinese friends, all the foreignness of China was put on hold in the glow of free expression—the adult version of the social excitement my young students exhibited each week.

Teacher, Student

I was in their country. So while I taught them my language, they taught me theirs. TPR offered their English teachers complimentary Mandarin classes twice a week. This was nice for obvious reasons, but also because it provided the perspective to see what it was like for my students: keeping up with what a fast-talking teacher says, wrapping your head around the new grammar and vocabulary, and demonstrating your know-how in front of your fellow pupils when called upon in class.

Tiffany, a twenty-four-year-old native Guangdonger, was our teacher. She was good natured, mellow, and happy.

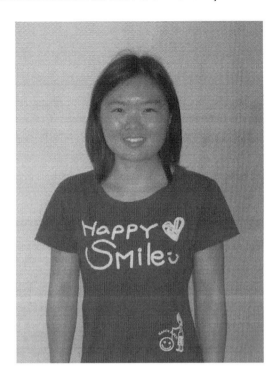

The hardest part about learning a language isn't the memorization—it's the shift in thinking, or perhaps the "being" Mandarin, Spanish, Arabic, or whichever language you study. Actually, thinking became a liability for me when trying to converse in Mandarin. It reminded me of learning a dance—you pick up some moves/words and get by with this rote recital for a little while. But when you want to take your skills to the next level, you realize you have to stop recalling memorized lines and start knowing and "flowing" the language—going from thought to being.

I worked at it and would attain a basic level of Mandarin. Classes were indispensable for vocabulary and practice, but what really got me to new heights of foreign language fluency was circumstantial learning. I always remembered what a seven-year-old boy exclaimed on one of my early days teaching. I took away his toy in class and he reached back for it from his desk exclaiming, "Gěi wǒ!" Given the context and emotions surrounding his plea, I could attach the sounds coming out of his mouth to something that stuck. The boy wanted his toy back.

"Give me!" he said.

***

Meet the Parents

As part of my teaching duties, I was asked to attend a "Joy Family Night" (labels were always so literal in China). For this event, a student's family would host their teacher for dinner. I wasn't sure if it was something my school did to impress their clients or what the parents did to benefit their child's education, but off I went on a Saturday night.

After classes ended on that Saturday in early November, two twenty-something female staff members of the school and I arrived with a couple gifts at the door of the residence on the sixteenth floor. It was an apartment, and believe it or not, the fact that a middle class family of four lived here rather than a house marked the most surprising difference between their lifestyle and that which I knew in America. (I had anticipated the language and food bridges to cross.) Indeed, turns out the biggest surprise was how "at home" I felt.

The father opened the door and welcomed us into the small entry area with a coat closet. To the right was the living room with a sofa and television. Further inside, the dining room was on the left and kitchen on the right. Further back still ran a hallway to the bathroom and two bedrooms. If you got rid of the Chinese characters on wall calendars and other décor, and maybe added a touch of color to the plain white walls, this apartment could belong in any of countless complexes in suburban America.

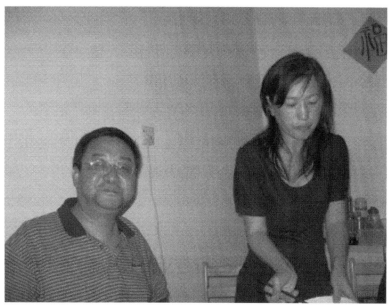

The King and Queen of this castle sitting in the dining room

The father's English was quite good, and after being seated, he shared with me his family's story. He's from northern China and met his wife in Beijing. They lived in Singapore for a few years (a tiny country straight south of China near the equator) and then Denmark for a few more before settling here in southern China. He is employed as an engineer; actually, he manages a team of engineers who were working their fingers to the bone designing the little vibrators in cell phones. He explained that with all the players in the marketplace and a steady turnover of new phones, competitors were breathing down their neck for every opportunity. So he was regularly at the office twelve hours a day.

The mother, as far as I knew, was a stay-at-home mom. They had a nine-year-old daughter—my student whose English name was Minny—and a preschool-aged son, which obviously goes against the one-child policy.

[The one-child policy or "family planning policy" (jìhuà shēngyù zhèngcè, 计划生育政策) restricts urban couples to only one child, while allowing additional children in several cases, including twins, rural couples, ethnic minorities, and couples who both lack siblings themselves. (Wikipedia.org) Also, urban couples can have another child, but will have to pay a fee based on their income, and, from what others in China told me, civil workers—police, teachers—will lose their job.

As one might expect, the policy has had mixed results and prompted mixed reactions. According to Western estimates it has prevented the births of 100 million children (China estimates much higher). A population reduction is welcomed in China, but the avoidance of that second child (or the selection process for your only one) has led to live birth killings, selective abortions, and forced abortions. Because of this, in the 1980s the United States pulled funding from the United Nations Population Fund, which backs China's Family Planning Policy. In 2009, the US president resumed funding for the program.

Note: In November 2013, the Chinese government relaxed the policy by allowing families to have two children if one of the parents is an only child.]

Dad, being in the private sector, steered clear of losing his job, and I assume paid the fee for having his son. Yet even with the family size and resources, this middle-class family didn't reside within a four-bed, two-and-a-half bath sprawl. In Zhuhai, homes were expensive.

After small talk, we started to prepare for dinner. Or I should say, we started to *prepare* dinner. This wasn't just going to be a "feed the teacher" night. It was a participatory, get-to-know-you event that meal prep is wonderfully amenable to—particularly dumpling-making, a culinary/social tradition here in China that goes way back.

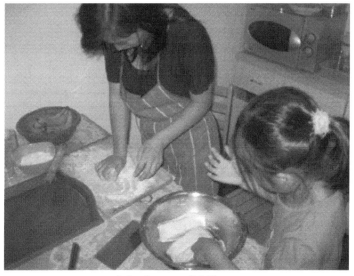

Mother and Minny

I got schooled in the art of dumpling making. We flattened balls of homemade dough into three-inch patties. Inside I put a pork-based filling (somehow greenish in color) and then pinched the dough closed. My first efforts were misguided by overestimating the amount of filling to use, making my dumplings more like *plump*lings. I also couldn't make the "sewn" endings come together in a pretty fingernail-indented row that the pros here could. But they were functional as they held together. Function, not form, right? Yeah, tell that to the engineer.

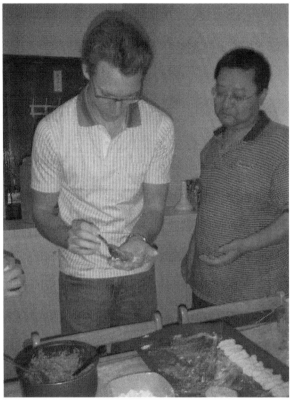

"Brandon, why don't you just give that to me."

I got the hang of it—sort of. There's an art to it, really. Eventually, I did get one to look picture-worthy.

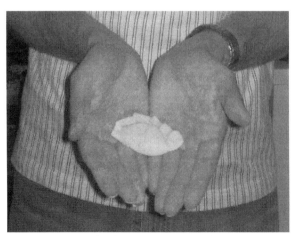

Dumplings as a side dish is common in Zhuhai, but according to Dad they make for a main course in the North. And tonight it was ours.

While the dumplings cooked, I played with Minny's little brother. As if to cater to the memory of my life back in Minnesota, I felt like I was with one of my own nephews.

Same games, different little boy

After using me as a road, I returned the favor by taking his little toy train and driving it around the floor, detoured it over his shoulder and onto his head. Next, we rammed toy cars together and completed a jumbo-pieced jigsaw puzzle.

Soon it was time to eat. We all sat around the table and ate dumpling after dumpling...after dumpling after dumpling after dumpling. Vintage Northern Chinese, said Dad. We chatted away, and I felt as comfortable and relaxed as if eating at another's home in my own country. I approached this night thinking there'd be some cultural or behavioral division between me and this family. Perhaps I'd eat the food the wrong way or something. (Perhaps I did.) But in a most intimate of settings, I felt welcome—from meal prep...

...to meal time.

I fit in like a glove, the world feeling comfortably smaller.

***

Wealth: Equalizer and Diversifier

As surprised as I was to experience the level of familiarity in my student's family's home, it was my students themselves who really took me aback.

I know an American man from India and an American woman from South Korea who on separate occasions shared with me the same experiences of traveling to their mother countries: people there could tell right away that they were American. Similarly, I expected something other than eyes and skin tone to differentiate the Chinese child from his or her counterpart in America—clothing, carriage, attitude, demeanor, expression—something bigger than any one thing and so encompassing it's hard to point out. But whatever this factor was (if I had to take a stab at it, I'd say it was their ease of expression), I'd find that on account it, my children students would blend right in back home in most classrooms...that is, until they opened their mouths.

During a speaking drill practicing the verb *to be* I said, "I am American," and they responded with, "I am Chinese." I went down the line from student to student repeating this. After the sixth or seventh student, I paused a beat and thought, "Hmm, these little buggers are Chinese."

I forgot.

The variables I could think of to account for this blend were prosperity, modernity, and globalization. These students lived in a city and came from families with enough extra income to afford these English classes. I assumed they had Internet and television at home by which they watched the latest media and trends. Once on this prosperity, modernity, globalization plane, it's interesting how universalized people become.

The counterbalance to this trend is that with more resources for self-expression, these individuals displayed much greater variety denoting their particular tastes. Thus, the idea that "all Chinese people look alike" seemed absurd in my classes.

Sometimes, though, there was an unfortunate familiarity that may have been assisted by China's growing prosperity. My class of eleven-year-olds had a real "this is boring and we're not going to go along with your stupid lesson" attitude. One day when trying to keep the attention of this hard-to-please group of fifteen students—some with eye-rolling expression—I remember thinking, "You little brats." Reynold told me one day that some of his students regularly called him fat and said unmentionable things about his mother. He knew the language, so he caught it all.

The thought occurred to me that having the best of both worlds—prosperity and contentment—requires enhanced discipline as the former increases. As the ability to appease oneself or one's children with more stimulation rises, so does the potential difficulty to realize that true happiness comes from things that can't be purchased. I guess this is a growing pain of a developing country.

***

Love Interest in China

The TPR branch I taught at each weekend shared bathroom facilities with an adjacent art school. So I walked through their hall each time Nature called. One time on my way to respond, nature interrupted herself with a different call—two of them, actually: the sounds of string and wood reverberation, and the sight of a beautiful woman making the music.

Between classes one weekend morning, I exited my school's reception area through the doorway connecting us to the art school's reception area. Past their entryway was the showroom with a mixture of Western and Eastern instruments: pianos, violins, guzhengs...

...and erhus.

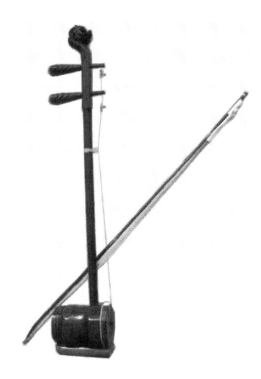

A hallway extended opposite the showroom floor—between practice rooms, an art studio where I'd see a teacher having his pupils draw a bowl of fruit, and a dance studio where I'd see young ballerinas. As I approached the hall I heard the twangy, soft intensity of the guzheng (*gǔ zhēng*, 古筝).

I looked through the tall, narrow window into the small practice room to see a teacher playing for her student. Not only were the deep, touching sounds a fitting soundtrack for her elegant looks, but her real-time musical creation showed that her delicate yet deliberate hands and wrists were as visually appropriate for this dreamy music as her beauty. She continued with her student, and I had to get back to class.

A week or two later, I walked by the room and noticed her inside by herself. I knocked, she answered, and I introduced myself. She had light skin and beautiful smile. She kept her hair back in a ponytail, revealing her soft eyes. I asked about the instrument, and she showed me. Her English was fairly good. I played on it a little bit. "That's good!" she said. From then on, I'd stop in while walking by, if she was present and free.

We started having lunch, and we even started helping each other with our respective languages. But music was the language we used best. One time I showed my skills by playing a couple beats in the drum set practice room. She was the courter with her music, though, once playing Bach's *Well-Tempered Clavier 24* on the piano. It felt as if the music revealed a new, deeper part of her— an expression that opened the door to intimacy.

Finally the day came, about a month after we met and two months into my stay in China, when we planned to see each other outside school hours. We met along that picturesque boulevard along the coast in the afternoon. It actually extends for miles all the way to Macau and is known as Lover's Walk. They say if you make the journey with your partner, you'll live happily ever after. Today it was just a meeting place.

We walked the same bridge out to that same little island Marilyn and I had circumnavigated my first days in Zhuhai. But instead of a tandem bicycle, we rented a go cart-like vehicle that had us sitting and pedaling side-by-side. The scenery, and the effort needed to tour it, was a great combination of place and activity for this date. We went halfway around the island and then decided to walk the trail to the top of the island hill.

Minus the pedaling, it was just us and our walk. I had still wondered about the intention of our time together—perhaps something was lost in our imperfect lingual compatibilities. But I also felt secure that affection was mutual. I took her hand. We got to the top and looked at the view. With the ocean and city visible through a break in the trees, I leaned toward her and kissed her. She kissed me back but only for a moment and then tilted her head down and away.

"What is it?" I asked.

She hesitated to say anything. I just had to wait and wonder—until she said:

"I'm engaged."

She then shared about her fiancé back in her home province. I was disappointed and frustrated, but more than anything, I knew what we had to do next. I told her we'd go back to being friends and act as if this had never happened. With that, we quietly walked back down, pedaled back with lessened excitement, and walked the bridge to the coast.

During the walk I asked, "If you have a fiancé back home, then why are you here with me?" Either she couldn't explain it in English—couldn't at all—or didn't want to. But her expression indicated she wasn't sure why she did. After that, we crossed paths here and there as friends. Each time I saw her, I felt a little sad.

Looking back, logistics and practicality would've have made a relationship difficult to maintain. But I lightened up on Heath and others whom I had judged for being in "less robust" relationships. My romantic and affectionate draw to this woman was quite strong, and had she not been engaged, I probably would've found myself in a similar relationship.

***

An American Holiday in China

Halloween is celebrated in China? That was my first reaction when seeing its merchandise for sale in stores. Well, I guess it makes sense that they soak in this example of America's high values and noble culture. After all, in a culture big on saving face, there's no better deed than donning a mask.

As he did when I first arrived, Navid asked me to participate in the celebration. It being Halloween, I at least had some idea this time about what to expect. Still, he never said what I'd be doing. Perhaps we'd be tossing toilet paper in the old neighborhood trees or something.

The event was held in a rotunda of a shopping center in the Jida neighborhood. In front of a slew of folding chairs stood an impressive stage and backdrop.

Filling the chairs were several parents with their costumed children. Meanwhile, participants and emcees prepared offstage.

My fellow rookie teachers, Marilyn and Reynold, joined me in the front row so to be ready for our participation. Perhaps our involvement would be as costume contest judges, but nope—three other veteran faculty members had that honor.

Esteemed panel

The audience of at least one hundred looked on as the emcees—two adolescent girls and one boy—opened the evening. They then introduced the first performers.

It had a pageant vibe as the girls danced with pasted-on smiles and moms made up their wee one's faces.

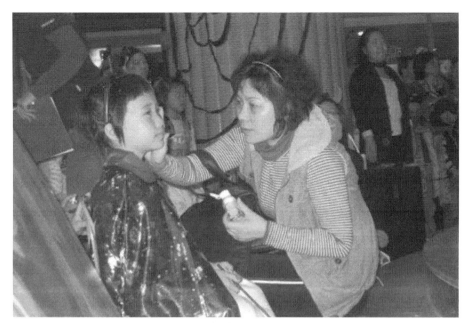

"Honey, maybe if you were going as a witch, but your wand-wielding bug/fairy get-up did not require a pimple."

After these girls was another performance, this one involving even younger children in a variety of costumes. It was chaotic: kids uncertain where to go, one crying, and parents encouraging them from the floor. In other words, it was great.

Next, it was time for the costume contest.

Wished I was the judge. I'd have voted for Boxboy.

Well, I wasn't. But I soon got my answer to why I came...

This final event had three sets of parent/child pairs walk up onstage. Reynold, Marilyn, and I were asked to jump up there with them, each matched with one of the parent/child combos. I accompanied a father and his ten-year-old boy. I still had no clue what for and hoped it didn't involve speaking because I couldn't say ten words to the dad.

"Lucky" for me, I wouldn't have to say a thing. In fact, there would soon be a moment when my mouth would be covered. For it was up to my teammates to mummify us teachers with toilet paper as fast as possible. I don't know if they understood the tie-in to the American Halloween tradition, but yes, I had to make like a tree and get TP'd.

3...2...1...Go!

Hectic music and a vocal audience matched the energy with which father and son scrambled around me. Looking over at my coworker, Reynold, I realized my guys weren't doing half bad.

Prior to coming here, I imagined a lot of different places to go, people to meet, and things to do—but this? I took it as testament to the interesting places life will take you. (Or perhaps it was just karma for complaining about bathrooms never having tissue.)

Although my guys did a good job, Marilyn's team took home the prize.

Actually, we all won, right? Free TP for the rest of the year!

***

It had been a memorable and rich first two months in China, but after a public TPing I needed a break.

Chapter Six: Western Respite #1: Macau

Zhuhai's proximity to Macau provided a convenient change of pace. I wanted to break the ice on this first visit by learning the history of this intersection point of East and West and checking out the unique Macanese culture. I got all that and a lot more.

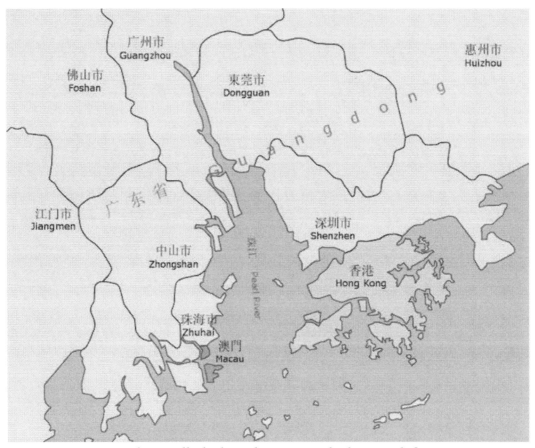

Macau is the small, darkened region in the bottom left-center.

What is this Macau place? Most people I talked to back home hadn't heard of it, and those who had knew very little. Macau itself is small—11.4 square miles (29.5 square kilometers). By comparison, Minneapolis is over five times the area. So what's the big deal about an area this small?

History.

Gambling.

Wealth.

First, the history. Macau was both the first and last Western colony in China, settled by Portuguese traders in the 1500s and ruled by Portugal all the way up until December 20, 1999. Certainly in that time a lot of changes took place, but not just cultural or societal. This region doubled in land area (you read that right) in just the last forty years to meet the demands of economic and population growth. Here's how a map of the region looked in 1986:

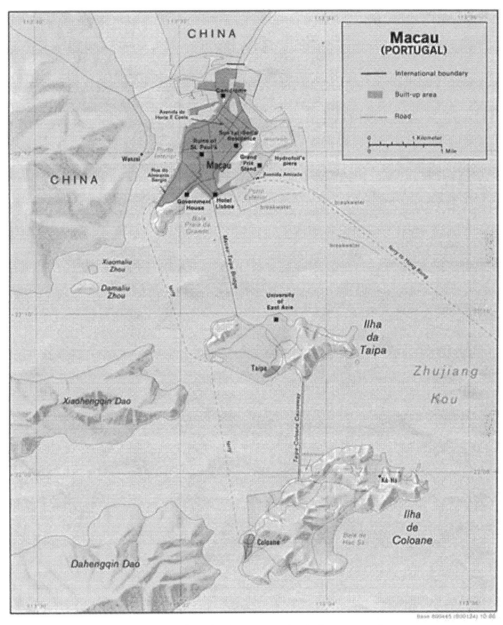

Zhuhai is the top center chunk of mainland China. Right below it is the Macanese Peninsula and its two small islands, Taipa and Coloane, totaling 6.4 square miles for all of Macau at the time.

Today, the region is made up of the peninsula, which is now bigger, but has been reduced to just one island.

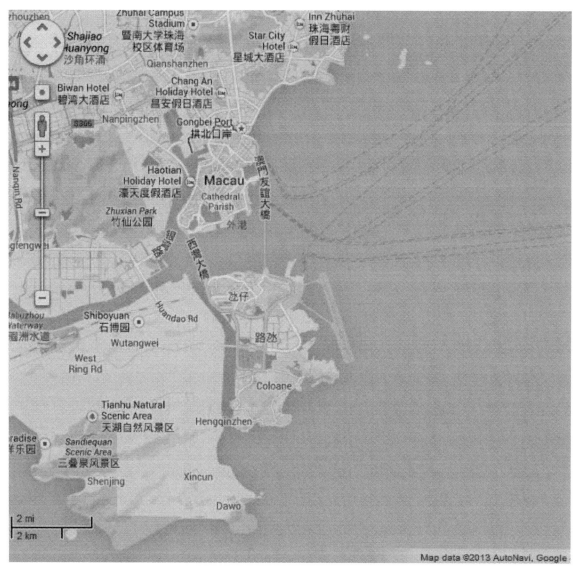

And two new bridges and an airport to the right—yet still only 11.4 sq. miles.

[You might wonder how this land "grew." Did the Earth's plates shift? Did water levels lower? Water didn't go down; land went up. Many, many loads of dirt were taken from nearby hills and dumped into the shallows. It's called land reclamation, and this was the first time I knowingly came face-to-face with this phenomena. As you can see from the two maps, mainland China has reclaimed a little land herself.]

I awoke early on this fall Saturday morning and took the bus straight for the border.

Gongbei Bordergate into Macau

The apartment buildings in the background of the picture and to the left are Macau—yet they are also still China. Like Hong Kong, which was handed back to China from the British in 1997, Macau exists in that brackish territory of being a Special Administrative Region (SAR). This arrangement is officially known as "One country, two systems" or *yī guó liǎng zhì* (一国两制) or, as said in Portuguese, *Um país, dois sistemas.*

The result is a region that maintains sovereign governance within the larger bubble that is China. In the case of Macau and Hong Kong this means more liberal economic and social policy. You can surf the Internet and worship freely. The currency is different, too: the Macanese *pataca.* And perhaps most obvious, people drive on the other side of the road. Both of these regions are also cleaner and wealthier than the mainland. So though one can see Macau's tall apartment buildings and even the towering casinos easily enough from southern Zhuhai, the contrasts between the two places (and the rigmarole of waiting in line and getting approval to cross into Macau) adds a foreign feel to it.

Inside Bordergate is a huge room with a lot of metal tubing used to divide lines of people, as seen at amusement parks. There were about twenty such long, straight lines facing border workers dressed in government whites and blues and seated behind glass on elevated counters. Like a grocery store checkout, the number of lines open depended on how busy it was. When a line opened to handle more traffic, I was impressed by how quickly the fifty-foot line filled with scurrying people. One at a time, we tourists made our way up and had our picture taken, handed over a customs form, and got our passport stamped.

I walked past security and through the wide, echoing hallway with the throng of others. Thousands and thousands cross each day—many for work (who have a special pass and special queue for efficient passage); others to buy goods—you can get some things in Macau that you can't get in mainland China; others—many others—who come to gamble for the day; and finally, those such as myself—foreigners who simply want to visit. Leaving the bland, livestock-like corridors of Bordergate, I exited to a fresh new environment.

The other side of the customs building greeted me with the old border gate: a tannish-yellow, stone-arched wall section with Portuguese etched into it. It looked like it belonged in Latin America and stood as a testament to the not-too-distant days when Portugal was in charge.

Also marking this influence was the Portuguese written on every official document: customs forms, street names, government buildings. It's quite useless these days, however.

Past the stone arch, a long fountain with vertically shooting jets welcomed me alongside the outdoor walkway running perpendicular to the border and main road up ahead. A place this small needs to get down to business quickly, and as soon as the walkway ended, there you were in the midst of traffic and pedestrians—many of them. Because of Macau's size and half-million people, it is the densest populated place on Earth.

Admittedly, this is a picture of a tourist area elsewhere in Macau and is the most packed I'd see it here—obviously, I mean how could you get anymore packed?

The east/west-oriented road hugging the border was crowded with clothing stores, a McDonald's, convenience stores, and money changers. The first thing I did was exchange my Chinese yuan into Macanese pataca, about a 4:5 ratio. Shooting south from this main drag were several streets leading into the heart of the Macanese Peninsula. Because tour buses hadn't yet started operating this early in the morning, I walked it. (And when I say tour bus, I mean casino bus. They function as free transportation to their slot machines and tables, but also work great for general transport to given areas.) My destination this morning was Senado Square (Senate Square), the old center of colonial Macau.

The busy border road quieted behind me with each passing step on my chosen southbound street, and things started to resemble my neighborhood in Zhuhai: a blend of apartments with small businesses in their base. I noticed the lack of debris on the streets, though, and recalled the videos they played on suspended televisions while I waited in line at Bordergate. They showed footage of a man tossing a cigarette butt with a red circle/slash symbol slamming atop the zoomed-in image of the cigarette, saying in effect, "No! You will not throw you butts on the ground in Macau!"

Anticipating Senado Square about a mile ahead, I had my destination put on hold when I looked to my left and noticed a temple. I hadn't yet seen such a place on the mainland. The Chinese people in Macau, under the protection of Portugal, escaped the rule of the Communists throughout the 1900s. Thus, temples and traditions were better kept. I didn't know anything about this temple, but saw from the outside that it was old yet maintained nicely. A stone exterior was topped with clay shingles and embellished with a pillared façade in front of its threshold. Before the building was a stone floor leading from the temple to where I stood on the sidewalk. A couple old trees poked through spaces in this floor of a front yard, and in the middle of it were two large, metal-sculpted incense burners.

I walked through the entrance, which revealed stone floors, wooden red-painted pillars, plants, and many hanging, smoking, coiled incense sticks. It was a cozy structure—the size of an average American home—but felt extraordinarily spacious as much of it was without a ceiling. Walking straight in, I headed for the main prize: an ornate altar. It had a gold-colored deity in the center against the red back wall. He sat upon his throne with a tall, flat-topped headpiece. Framing him were two columns and a top piece all covered in brown, gold, black, and teal-colored ornate wood work. Before the deity sat a table with urn and vases filled with sand in which dozens of incense sticks smoldered, emitting their aroma.

[Later I'd find out this is a Taoist temple called Lin Fung Miu: Temple of the Lotus. It was built in 1592 and renovated in 1752. Taoism is similar to Buddhism in that it emphasizes meditation and harmony with all that exists. One key difference, though, is in its worship of many gods whereas Buddhism has none.]

Off to the sides of this room, smaller altars sat with their own more humble calls for attention, and attention was paid, as freshly lit incense testified.

Within this space were plenty of other works to take in.

Good News: his ax is down. Bad News: his hand is raised, ready to give you an "awakener."

I felt the calm and call of my full attention to the beautiful and rich spiritual presence layered within these rooms by the countless practitioners that had been here before me.

This room was only the front half of this temple. Behind the altar was another space featuring a fountain.

Similar to the front room, this space had the same stone floors, suspended incense, and red wooden pillars. And it, too, featured a decorative altar at the front. This room was more musical, though. Along the side walls were two percussive instruments whetting my whistle and hearkening to my concert band playing days. A large, dense bell hung three feet off the ground with a swinging battering-ram mallet suspended next to it.

The gracious middle-aged man who worked at the temple gestured for me to go ahead and make some sweet temple music. As you would suspect, the heavy metal made a resounding "boooonnnnggggg." when struck. What I didn't expect was that when I did so, a local woman took the opportunity to add some resonance to her worship. At the sound of the bell, she knelt.

It was neat to see and be a part of the spiritual world here in Macau.

Then I looked across the room and saw another chance to make some meditative music.

The man said to strike the drum three times with the 18-inch batons resting together on the wall near the drum's base. Each echoed a deep thud.

After my percussive participation, I made a donation and thanked the workers for letting me visit and participate. They smiled back eagerly. For one last lap, I slowly and soundlessly wandered the cool, open-built structure. The stillness of sculptures looking down at me, the natural light, and the sight and smell of the incense had my soul both at attention and at ease. I exited ready for the rest of the day.

The residual temple mood sharpened my view of the outside world—cars, signs, buildings, trees. I was energized to enjoy some historic sites at Senado Square. But once again, I was called to a detour. Just a block or two south, I happened to look through an open door up against the sidewalk directly to my left. The interior of this room was an unremarkable grey from floor to ceiling, but the items on the wall caught my attention.

Black and white headshots, one on each door

Since Macau is so crowded, I took these to be compartments for ashes. But a closer look revealed they weren't doors, but simply plaques to recognize lost loved ones. My attention was drawn to one woman's face.

Sometimes when I'm out and see a real old person, I imagine them in their youth. Seeing their child or young adult selves moves me, and I'm not sure why. I want to say it's the power and beauty of life, its transformational process, its brevity. Perhaps it's just a deep-seated fear of death. Here before me was Cristina, who, once fresh from the womb, is now gone—a pile of ashes.

What does one do with this mortal realization? It's intimidating and too vast to stay conscious of—yet it's always right there. Buddhists recognize that the key to happiness is the understanding and awareness that life is change. They say we can better appreciate life—be better at being in tune with the flow of change—if we recognize its temporary nature. I'll confess that when I feel this truth, it hurts to know that I will get old and I will die.

Despite any fear I have about this, my heightened awareness allowed an appreciation for Cristina. Engaged with her image, I imagined her whole life—her childhood, parents, family, holidays, dreams, lovers, passions, hobbies. I realized then the richness in all our lives. A thought followed: "Couldn't we all be more loving and patient toward one another knowing that each human is a vessel for such incredible activity?"

Cristina's life and death provided this exhalation of insight, breathing life into a deeper self.

Exiting, I continued south down the same road. It had been quite a morning already, having wandered the halls of a temple built to respect the realms of another life and then spending time in this room honoring the lives of those who've passed this one. With the resultant serenity and gratitude, I aimed for Senado Square.

After just a couple minutes walking on the same left side of the street, however, I encountered a driveway interrupting a seven-foot wall along the sidewalk. The driveway rose a few yards and spread out into a larger parking area. I can't recall what pulled me into this place, but I wandered in. At the top of the incline I saw a hearse parked straight ahead on the opposite end of the parking lot. Surrounding the lot were spaces for funeral services.

One service was in progress in the space to my left. I found a seat at the back of four rows of folding chairs that faced the altar. Above it hung a picture of the recently deceased gentleman. To the left of the altar sat half a dozen attendees in white, martial-arts uniforms.

Martial arts men are in the back near the altar. This man is bowing toward a Buddha statue.

Separating the rows of folding chairs in which I sat was a yellow-clothed table with three brown-robed women chanting, with that small Buddha statue at its head.

They voiced the same incantation the entire twenty minutes I was there. I don't know the words, but the rhythm was: "quarter, quarter, quarter, quarter, half....half..." over and over and over. One held a high-pitch bell which she struck for every repetition.

I think these women were recognizing the transition from this world to the next. And I'd like to think they were exercising their own existential realizations. But if half of what funerals are about is clarifying your life, the other is to honor the one just gone:

I looked at the picture of the man being honored. I then asked that this lost life continue to help motivate better living here on Earth. It was—as suggested by those who were in attendance, as felt by me.

Culminating this morning, I felt motivated to acknowledge and smile at the people I pass on the street, to embrace the moments I have with my nephews, and by all means, to resist getting wrapped up in less important matters. It's actually pretty cool to think that this man had some American guy come sit in on his funeral and walk away a better person. I bet he never thought that would happen.

After a few more minutes, I rose to leave, unsure how to proceed. Architecture and colonial history seemed so worldly all of a sudden. But I also realized the meditative and spiritual are wrapped together with the educational and enjoyable. The former births our ability to satisfy the latter. Deepening my roots makes it all the better for my such branches to reach new heights. So I resumed my original plan, this time without detour.

By now, the neighborhood had evolved. More than the mere cleanliness distinguishing it from my own was a cosmopolitan air.

Western-looking street clock in the center—I was nearing Senado Square.

Government buildings, a large stone fort, and churches decorated this section of town, just as these types of buildings do in many former colonies around Asia, Africa, and Latin America.

Surrounding Senado Square itself were colorful, pillared, and arched structures around a plaza of black and white-striped brickwork making an architectural exclamation.

Colonial with a Chinese flare

I followed the black-and-white bricked surface between spectacular buildings and under flower-shaped lanterns whose light I imagined would be dazzling come nightfall.

Even under a cloudy day, this plaza was a real bright spot.

Back through this corridor the showy was replaced by the ordinary: narrow streets and alleys bordered by small restaurants, shops, and apartments.

So cozy compared to Minneapolis; so clean compared to Zhuhai.

I had a freshness and lightness exploring these new blocks. Each step was a firm grip on the sidewalk aided by an accompanying flow that had me glide from block to block. And this was despite the route getting awful hilly.

I kept ascending the quiet streets until I reached the next site on this walking tour: Monte Forte (Mount Fortress).

Monte Forte is a Jesuit creation from over four hundred years ago.

I walked up the path, reached the entryway, and followed the pathway inside that ramped up to the plane on which those cannons rested.

Only twice did they have occasion to fire these things. In one famous record, a Portuguese Jesuit was able to get off a perfect shot, landing the cannonball in the Dutch's gunpowder supply. Kaboom.

Two-and-a-half years prior, I had been in the historic tropical coastal city of Malacca, Malaysia. This was another Portuguese-founded colony (1511), but one that was conquered by the Dutch, then England, and finally handed back to the Malaysian state in 1946.

In both Malacca and here in Macau, I stared at the sea from atop their respective forts. I imagined when built, these were the tallest things around. Below these structures sat wood/stone buildings that livestock moseyed past, a local beside them on muddy roads. So far from home the invaders were! I'm sure they wished for a way to reach family in Portugal to tell them how different life was in these new worlds separated by all that water. I myself had this urge in 2010. Thankfully, I had a blog.

These ports represented the beginning of a new age of East/West connectivity, of lasting ties between these two great human trajectories. But despite their previous isolation, the East and West saw great parallels in their social development leading up to Portuguese landfall. This was demonstrated here at Monte Forte where, in its center, was a history museum matter of factly named the "Museum of Macau."

As I entered from the top of the fort, the first exhibit was a hallway display encompassing this idea of Eastern and Western trajectories. Each side of the corridor represented their respective social evolutions up through time until the emergence of the seafarers of the 1500s. On the right-hand side, the glass-fronted display showed how the West philosophized from the inspiration of Socrates. Meanwhile, the left side of the hallway countered with its own display showing how the Chinese did so inspired by Confucius. A couple steps forward and the West worshipped Jesus, while on the left, the East found spirituality in Taoism and Buddhism. On it continued. When the West birthed Beowulf, the Chinese offered Romance of the Three Kingdoms or *Sān Guó Yǎn Yì* (三国演义). And when the West played the lyre, China played the guzheng.

This hallway—maybe thirty feet long—revealed, objectively and architecturally, how these two great societies developed in parallel fashion. It spoke to a fundamental common ground of all humanity, yet also the specifics of each, which indicate all that we can teach/learn from one another. It helped me appreciate the monumental achievement of Portugal's permanent contact with China, and how this meeting shaped the future even to eventually allow me to stand where I was.

This hallway was just the warm-up to this museum. Moving on offered many more exhibits, such as a large wall display of the map of the world. Small light bulbs decorated this map by dotting ancient seafaring trade routes connecting Europe to the East. In other areas of the museum, the expected displays of art and religious artifacts were featured, as well as impressive, unexpected domestic mock-ups showcasing old-school life for native, pre-industrial Macanese.

My brain bucket full of knowledge, I left the fort to finish up the historical tour with its most popular attraction.

The Ruins of St. Paul's

Built in the late 1500s by the Jesuits, the Cathedral of St. Paul was once one of the crowning religious achievements of the colonial world. After a typhoon and subsequent fire in 1835, however, this landmark became known as the Ruins of St. Paul's or *Dà sān bā Pái fāng* (大三巴牌坊) or, in Portuguese, *Ruínas de São Paulo*. I thought it funny how after the storm and fire, they just never got around to cleaning up what was left of the church. But now its façade is an attraction with much to tell about the days of old: religious symbols used, Asian/European architectural influence, and Portugal's power.

Leaving the ruins behind, I set my sights on a return home, so walked to the nearest casino. I stepped inside the pristine and colorful rooms and halls—a tease for a future visit—so I could get home. I hopped aboard their bus transport back to the border, then made my way back through Bordergate. I waited in line, got my passport stamped—this time by a Chinese worker in light green garb—and returned to my "real life" in Zhuhai, a little wiser about human history, and, recalling my morning, a little wiser about human life.

Chapter Seven: China on the Street

Blood, Slime, Fur, Feathers

The wet market (as we English-speakers dubbed it) was quite the filet of Chinese life, and it made quite a statement of man's interaction with animal.

My alarm woke me up earlier than I was used to this November morning. It was early for me because I'm no fisherperson, or fish-salesperson, or even much of a fish-buyer. But that's when the fish come in from the boats. (It always seems like anything to do with fish or game requires such early hours). So today I needed to wake up with the fishes to check out the wet market just three blocks from my apartment here in old downtown Zhuhai.

I walked outside in the jacket weather and approached the wet market building, a concrete stronghold. Decorating the outside were men in black, water-proof aprons pushing carts of Styrofoam containers and blue plastic totes filled with water and sea creatures. Entering the market floor reminded me of a flea market—an expansive, open area with smooth floors and florescent lighting. Rows of tables weren't covered with knickknacks, though, but with shallow basins filled with seafood over which people dickered and bickered across, passing bills from dry hand to wet, slimy hand.

After taking in the ambiance, I focused in on specifics. The animals for sale were as interesting to look at as they were to imagine consuming.

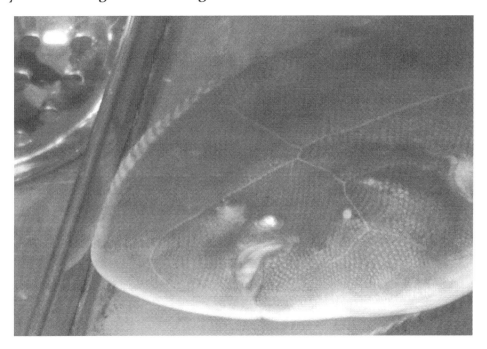

The vendor hadn't seen this escapee, so I said, "Hey man, your eel's making a slither for it."

Then, things here went from fishy to reptilian.

All alive and looking for a home.

Next were these odd turtles:

This soft-shell variety had their penetrable shells poked through near their tail for a string to leash them in place. Watching them trying to walk away while affixed had me feeling bad for them.

How does one keep frogs from hopping away?

Apparently, by binding them in groups.

Or just use a net...

...or, better yet, a basket.

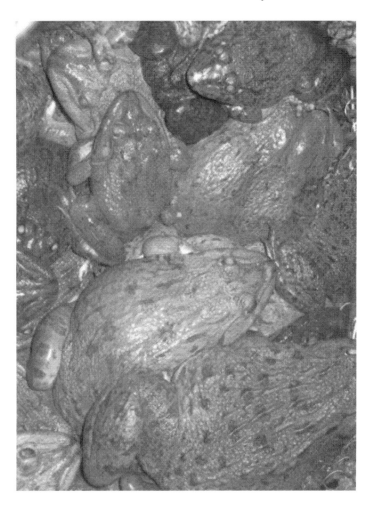

While someone brought the animals here, others worked on them. Butchers prepared their product for waiting customers—chopping off fish heads, slicing steaks of the larger fish, and scaling the smaller ones.

Meanwhile, we silly Minnesotans throw out our delicacy walleye heads.

I watched another young worker spend a long time in the "catcher" position, squatting and skinning eel-like creatures upon a long, thin board.

I also watched a woman take a pair of scissors and deal with the leg-bound frogs by snipping off the front half of their heads. Finally, another woman took catfish one by one and ended their lives in the humane fashion of beating their skulls with a wooden mallet.

It was the simple sight of seeing a guy mindlessly toss live frogs into a bucket as indifferently as if they were plastic, toy ones that cracked my armor to realize the cruelty—if you wish to call it that—that took place here.

I remember thinking, "Hey Man, take it easy on them toads."

However, I thought it was hypocritical to say that animals deserve to be treated better when I eat meat all the time—even intending to buy some here. The apathetic toad-tosser's treatment took away any sugar coating from the human designation of these animals as commodities. And seeing the slaughter right out in the open reminded me that we do a good job in the West of masking and ignoring what goes on behind the menu. By witnessing all the captivity, escape attempts, and the mechanism of animal harvesting, I realized it would be ideal to not have to interfere with all this life.

But I also wasn't convinced that either you toss frogs or you let them go. There can be a tie between consumption and increased respect. I see this most regularly from hunters and fishermen back in Minnesota, where the act of seeking out the animal heightens the appreciation for it and incentivizes the sportsman to see the species flourish. I've seen farmers show a similar respect for their livestock. In the face of necessity, practicality, or just enjoyment, there's a respect for the living creatures both despite and because of reliance on them. On the other end of the spectrum is the business of animal harvesting and the efficiency that comes with treating animals purely as products.

I then thought that since this kind of moral tightrope is only as required as our need to kill animals, the answer lies in removing that need. Synthetic leather and fur are common; meat substitutes are improving; and cultivating meat outside the animal is in the works. If these technologies become common and affordable, we won't have to live the contradiction of killing the animals we love. I liked where this was headed. But my next realization was that this doesn't really solve anything on a grand scale because eating/using animal resources is just one example of how humans butt heads with other species. We kill countless critters when a bridge or home is built. To maximally save animal life, we'd have to park the car, lest we hit a bug on our windshield. We'd have to stop walking the sidewalks full of anthills. In the end, I realized life is a vehicle used by all species in constant interaction and competition. The line of morality, then, seems to exist within the realm of living a "reasonable" life and—barring any special exception for, say, endangered species—being okay with animals perishing on account of that.

Being here also prompted thoughts about humans' animal hierarchies. Most people I know value mammals more than reptiles. Insects are completely expendable. It seems the level of perceived closeness to an animal species determines where our ideas of cruelty begin. With this comes a window of edible acceptability—if intimacy with a species is low, many want little or nothing to do with them. Thus, eating insects and reptiles is considered exotic, daring, and perhaps even gross and wrong.

Cockroach salad in Cambodia

"Not cool," say most people I know.

On the other end of the scale—dog, horse—many have similar reactions but for opposing reasons.

Dog in Vietnam: "Not cool," say most people I know.

Finally, in the middle is the Goldilocks region: just right. So bring on the cow, deer, pig, and duck.

Outside the market was the furry and the feathered. I exited the east side of the building to an alley lined with small storage-like units. Within them held all sorts of surprises. Right away I watched one young man open one and reveal what he had.

The spray paint on the forehead indicated something.

Further along the alley were cages of ducks, geese, and other fowl I hadn't seen before—most of them packed like sardines. The scene was straight out of the evening news when they do a story on the Avian Bird Flu. I heard—then saw—a goat crying as it was bled for slaughter. Next I saw another recently deceased one being torched to rid it of all its hair.

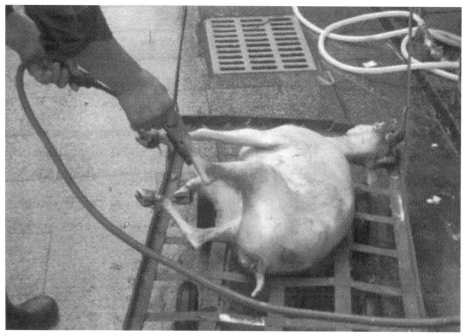

Aw man, right in the joey-makers. I admit my own bias towards the mammals and the difficulty hearing a goat cry its final breath. Fish don't vocalize. Perhaps it's arbitrary and silly; perhaps it's logical given that I'm a mammal, too.

To wrap up my morning, I went back inside the market to buy some food for dinner plans that evening with Reynold and a couple Chinese friends. I thought about all the new things to try but wasn't in a daring mood, so I settled on shrimp and crab. That night, seeing the results of all the labor and commerce from the fishing boat to the market to the kitchen added depth and appreciation to the meal.

Visiting the market was one part fascinating and invigorating, one part troubling, and one part thought-provoking. I decided that as long as I do keep eating meat, the best thing I can do to respect the sacrifice of the animal is to use its energy and nourishment to live a productive life of my own. It's no consolation to the animal, but gratitude and respect will help me find the right balance in my own human/animal interplay.

***

Macau had inspired me to better appreciate others by acknowledging the richness of people's lives. Soon after, two individuals in Zhuhai helped me appreciate enrichment in two specific areas: skills and possessions.

Focusing On All That You *Can* Do

It's a wonderful place to be when one sees and focuses on their "cans." This was powerfully evident when an individual with such a blatant disability did so.

On a morning in late November, I was walking the backstreets of my neighborhood and passing the usual small eateries, shops, and locals, when up ahead on a corner, I noticed a crowd of about a dozen locals. As I approached them, I made out the centerpiece: a thin man dressed in a white tank top and dark slacks standing barefoot over a half-dozen, spread out, large red sheets of paper. Oversized handwritten Chinese characters were artistically drawn on the sheets in black ink. One assumed he was the artist. But if that was the case, these handwritten characters were created by someone without arms.

"Holy cow!" I thought, taken aback upon seeing him. I had never seen an amputee so revealed.

My immediate next thought—so fast it was hard to catch—was, "How horrible life would be without arms." Crazy how automatic these fear-based thoughts are. I'd like to say it was sympathy—feeling bad for him. But it wasn't. Sympathy was just a conscious mask I put over my real feeling: fear and my wish to stomp it out by then asking, "Quick, where can I give him money?!" But hold on there, cowboy. This man wasn't looking for something-for-nothings. I hit the pause button of my mind to watch him perform.

He nudged his seat pad into place with his ankle and squatted down upon it. Though many people were watching, none helped. He clamped the red paper sheet to a cardboard backing with his nimble toes, then grabbed the paintbrush between big and second toe, dipped it in the ink can, and got to work.

After each few characters he'd have to realign: stand up, kick his seat over, and hunch back down.

Watching for just a minute, I wanted to give for an entirely different reason. So I did—as had many others.

By resisting my fear-backed urges for a pity-payment, my thoughts turned to admiration—first for his effort and output and then for something much deeper and in opposition to my knee-jerk reaction: fearlessness.

He wasn't begging; he was creating. He wasn't sorry; he was overcoming. And more than causing me to initially misinterpret this situation, I recognized this same fear-led perspective as the culprit having me focus on my "cannots" instead of my "cans." I feel inferior to Reynold because his Mandarin Chinese is better than mine; I feel lower than the man who can salsa dance better than I. This man's example before me, on the other hand, was a lesson for basking in the light of capability.

As a group of male onlookers quietly talked amongst themselves, this man's performance was the glue holding this social circle together. Others like me were passersby. But he paid little attention to the public except with a brief "xiè xie" when someone dropped a bill.

At some point in his past, this man (perhaps when yet a boy) decided to live rather than simply exist.

He demonstrated that the human spirit and the drive to express can overcome so much. The question I had walking away was, if armlessness can't stop the painter, what's ever stopping me from expressing myself?

At the Mercy of Others

It's not just "cans" and "cannots" people wrestle with, but—regarding possessions—their "dos" and "don'ts."

On my way to Mandarin class on a fair, early-December day, I came upon an individual I had previously seen a few times around my neighborhood. Each time, this person (man or woman I couldn't yet tell) just lay on his or her stomach on the sidewalk, head cocked out to face the passersby with a tin can nearby for alms. I once caught how this handicapped person got around when I saw a man lift him or her off a platform from his three-wheeled bicycle, lay the immobile middle-ager on their back on the sidewalk while he prepared a bed of blankets, and when he was done, rolled this person over to begin their day.

On this particular day, he/she lay out in the sun in loose-fitting blue sweater and navy sweatpants, and I planned on speaking to him/her after my class. When class finished, I asked Tiffany, our Mandarin teacher, to help translate. Though surprised to find out to whom we'd be talking, and a bit hesitant, she was still willing. Thankfully, so was this person on the sidewalk.

Her name was Jiang Ai Lan. She said she was fifty to fifty-five years old, adding that she couldn't remember clearly. She told us she was born with a condition that caused her inability to walk. Her arched back revealed her tanned, weathered face with a mop of grey, toussled hair atop.

And her position caused a strained effort to tell her story, which she nonetheless seemed eager to share.

Jiang had been lying around Zhuhai for the previous three years, but had been in the area for about twenty. She came from Hunan, the adjacent province to the north. That is where she met her husband, the man who sweeps her off her feet every day. They have a son in the fourth grade. (I was curious about conception and birthing, but didn't ask.)

2

After conversing for fifteen minutes, Jiang's husband happened to arrive. The small-statured man was named Sun Bao Cheng. He was fifty-four and, like his wife, was happy to talk. Interestingly, he said she was forty-seven, then he shared with us their daily routine. Every morning he drops his wife off around eight o'clock. She remains there for about three hours with nothing but the isolation of stationary begging. A couple times a day he moves her to a new spot. He also lunches with her. (Another time I walked by seeing him feed her noodles.)

In between his time with her, he said, he goes out and rummages through garbage—looking for valuables or recycling material, I'm guessing. At around six o'clock in the evening he picks her up, and they go home which was described as a space with blankets on the concrete. They do have some chairs, which they say their son uses to sleep along at night. They have no shelter, he said.

I asked if there's any place they can turn to for help. He said no. I asked him if he's had to resort to theft. He gave an emphatic no. Unfortunately, thievery has gotten the best of them, though, Jiang claiming that her can had been pillaged more than once.

Jiang, money can, and family transport

I asked how much money they had in the can—around twenty yuan. I cleared it out and replaced it with one pink 100RMB note. Sun gratefully pocketed it so that it wouldn't be stolen. Finally, he demonstrated how he carries her on and off his bike. One wonders how long he can keep up this lifting.

Given China's recent ascent toward prosperity, I wondered what individuals here were doing to help those less fortunate. To my surprise, I found that reaching out to help strangers wasn't all that normal in "One China" China.

Once on the bus, a pickpocket made an attempt on my bag. I found out only because a girl told me after we both got off at the same stop. In America, people might very well say something as they witness the activity. But from my experience—and from what fellow teacher Steve told me—the tendency in China is to keep mum. Throughout Tiffany's and my interview, several pedestrians stopped to watch. I'm sure the strangeness of the interview was enhanced because I was American. But putting aside this foreigner factor and acknowledging it's not exactly an everyday occurrence to interview beggars in any country, I think interest was strong because this wasn't something they'd think to do.

On our way to interview Jiang, Tiffany said plainly, "We don't do this."

"Do what?" I asked.

"Talk to people like this," she responded.

But we did today.

Then in my adult class, I brought up the topic of giving to beggars. Half the class expressed skepticism and caution. A couple said that many beggars fake their injuries or situations. A couple others gave the "enabling laziness" argument for not giving. One Chinese man, a former Salvation Army worker in Australia, said that some beggars—disabled or not—are part of a ring working for a "pimp" who organizes the circuit. Finally, I had people in and out of class talk about charity being a role for government. In one instance, a co-worker and I spoke to a TPR manager about starting a fund to teach English in remote areas of China. The manager warned us of the difficulty of charity, however. "That's the Party's job," she said—not as a matter of ideology, but simply as a matter of fact.

Though I've only traveled to a handful of different countries, from what I've heard, read—now experienced in China—I gained a fresh appreciation for the spirit of charity that thrives in America. Governmental spending on foreign aid is relatively low, but individuals more than pick up the slack, tripling what their European counterparts donate to domestic and global causes.

All this said, no one here in China was dying in the streets. I'd see the same beggars, and there were always enough random acts of charity to keep them coming back. Or, as exemplified by the armless painter, I'd see how the disabled came up with ways to earn. It wasn't what I was accustomed to, but I tried not to judge. It's hard to understand the scenarios that present themselves in a foreign land and the customs and traits that locals live by. Who knows? Maybe Jiang didn't have a son. Maybe that man wasn't her husband but rather the described "pimp" using this disabled woman as part of his operation.

As many wrinkles as this topic had, there were opportunities to give.

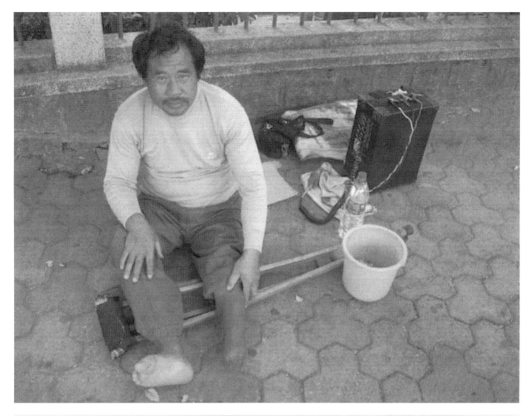

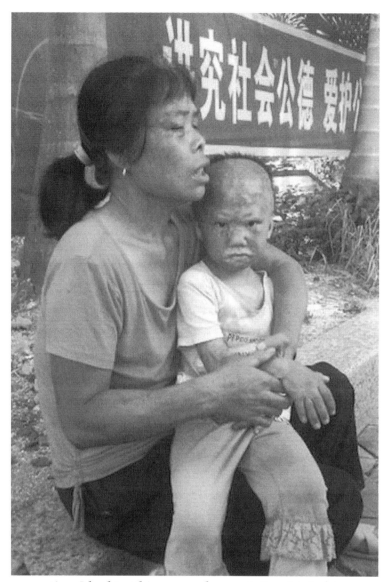

Despite the obvious reaction I had to this young burn victim, I tried to remember that the best thing I can do is offer love and positivity (along with a donation, perhaps). Then, do what I can in my own little way to help move humanity to a day where more people have more opportunity to make better lives for themselves.

Reminiscent of the painter, the following young woman created art despite—or perhaps because—of her disability: her crooked feet.

There were also healthy street performers.

This takes us to my next conclusion.

***

Everyone's an Entrepreneur

Prior to arrival I had known China as a communist country. And while seeing private enterprise didn't surprise me, I was surprised by the scale of it. The practice of free capitalism was how half the people seemed to make their living—albeit mostly at the street level. But even on higher rungs of the business ladder, the market operated with more freedom than I had previously thought.

My school was a private business founded and owned by Simone and his brother. Simone was a fortyish, portly gentleman about five feet nine inches tall, with a clean-shaven face and scalp. He and his brother purchased the four-story former bank building near my apartment to convert into TPR's headquarters and one of its branches. TPR also owned a seven-story office building in the Jida neighborhood that housed the Jida school branch plus the offices of other companies. In addition, TPR rented space in a few other locations in Zhuhai that were adequately sized for branches of three to six classrooms. In all, they had five branches around town and a few scattered in other cities of the Pearl River Delta. Navid shared with us in training that plans were in the works—plans that have since come to fruition—for more branches in more neighboring cities and communities. Such growth and development was the stuff mainly of American dreams, I thought.

Simone speaking at a staff event

At this staff event, I asked Simone, "How can communism allow for private property and enterprise?" Though I knew the economy had been liberalized somewhat, I still assumed you had to ask the government for everything. He answered plainly that twenty years ago he wouldn't, and couldn't, have done this. But things are different today. "That's old China," he said.

Commerce, as well, seemed to be defined by the individual entrepreneur. As much a statement about what people would do to make a living, the product-specific salespeople revealed the nature of a market place that supported these one-man operations. Department stores didn't dominate commerce, so for most non-food items I patronized independent outlets. This wasn't a moral decision but a practical one. Even most versions of shopping malls here featured several little independent vendors as opposed to the complexes of corporate chains I was used to seeing in America. This was best exemplified at The Underground Market that Heath first showed me my second day in China.

Everyone being an entrepreneur meant things were less corporate, which meant prices were negotiable. In fact, dickering was mandatory in the Underground Market to avoid being ripped off. Foreigners are a target. And though fun and novel to wheel-and-deal at first, it got old having to go through the rigmarole of hearing an abhorrent asking price, offering them much less, and then meeting in the middle. One of my first purchases was a couple ping-pong paddles and balls from a sporting goods stall. Later, I got an Internet camera from a tiny electronics vendor. There were a few others. And for some of these purchases, "meeting in the middle" meant knocking down the price a full two-thirds. Negotiations took place with facial expression and a big-buttoned calculator they all had.

Above the ground was a similar representation of salespeople. In one commerce-filled alley, the chopstick lady stood behind a large table with buckets filled with different varieties of shape, size, and color. Across the alley from the chopstick lady was the guy selling a few baby turtles and turtle food; the wall decal lady sat next to him. The fake Crocs footwear fellow also set up shop there each day. A Chinese friend told me that every brand name you see for sale on the streets (footwear, clothing, watches, handbags) is a knock-off.

Although Chinese laws prohibit unlicensed commerce and/or products, Zhuhai seemed to enact a "soft enforcement." I'd even sometimes see uniformed men walking amongst the vendors as any other citizen would. It seemed the whole culture helped promote this market: no social safety net, a low level of something-for-nothing attitude, and little enforcement of the laws. Only once all year did I see street vendors skedaddle from my neighborhood as enforcement arrived. In this case, they were selling food.

One rogue sales operation just two blocks from my apartment was so brazen that it rented out a large retail space. Outside their wide-open, garage-like front door, they blared Chinese pop dance music to attract walkers to come in and check out their impressive collection of DVDs. I'd like to see where they make these knock-offs. The DVD case cover sleeves were identical to the real thing, printed with the same high-quality glossy images and text. The only giveaways were the typos in the movie description on the back.

The youth exhibited this entrepreneurial spirit, too. All it took to make a little money was a small stand, a product, and a busy sidewalk. At night I saw (and patronized) a young guy—perhaps eighteen years old—setting up a one-man cell phone screen protector sale and service. He took my phone, removed the clear plastic from the screen, shaped up a new one on his little carving station, and adhered the new one with his makeshift wood/duct tape tool. Good as new. Five or ten yuan. Then when the night petered out, he'd pick up and go home—or maybe out with his night's earnings. Also at night, I witnessed on a couple occasions an after-dark sales blitz where a couple young guys unloaded a bunch of shoeboxes and then loudly declared their great deals, attracting onlookers to examine the goods.

All these micro-market players allowed for fluid and organic creation and movement. When the city opened the pedestrian underpass (pictured below) underneath the main road near the branch I taught at on weekends, those on foot were forced to cross underground. Guess who's waiting in the tunnel? Out came the sales sharks: a lady with baby clothes (I bought some for my niece); the guy with nothing but a cartload of papayas; a lady with ears of corn; and another merchant with small electronics. I wondered how they got their goods and what sort of distribution network exists behind these scenes.

Soon, though, things here did come to an end. In just a couple weeks, police stood guard, leaving this an empty cave.

Meal service also came in similar style.

There were many like him providing their portable provisions where it best served pedestrians.

I had to hand it to this guerilla capitalism maneuvering into the nooks and crannies of opportunity, a demonstration of people's creativity and service.

***

Capitalism's muscles were something I did expect to see flexed at my next destination and second Western respite.

Chapter Eight: Western Respite #2: Banking on Hong Kong

Walking back from Jusco, I passed by a bank. It wasn't the bank I used, but I entered to see if it would be okay to get some Chinese yuan exchanged into Hong Kong dollars. I'd be traveling there in just two days time.

Just about all Chinese banks are state-run. They have names like Bank of Communications, Bank of Agriculture, or the ubiquitous Bank of China. There are provincial-run banks, too, such as this particular one I stepped foot into: Guangdong Development Bank. Outside many banks sit two lion statues—one on each side of the doorway. Inside, banks look similar to those back home, except carpeting, coffee, and woodwork are replaced by white walls and white-tiled flooring. They evoke a feeling not unlike American DMVs or post offices and actually do a nice job of representing Chinese institutions as a whole—similar, but not quite as comfortable as their counterparts in America.

The tellers, typically younger women, wore uniforms of business skirts and blouses, their black shiny hair done up in a bun. Men were typically the bankers. One of these guys helped me as I walked in and responded to my request by saying it would be fine to perform this transaction. "Great," I said, and I left planning to get this done the following day. Twenty-four hours later, with wad of cash in hand, I entered and was grateful to see the same guy. We sat down, I provided my passport, and he started in with the paperwork.

After a few minutes, I took the paperwork and walked over and took a number from the ticket dispenser. In another few minutes I saw my number blinking above a teller. I approached and said: *"Wǒ yào Hong Kong qián"* ("I want Hong Kong money.") She nodded and fiddled on the computer. So far, so good. But as she typed I watched her expression morph from concentration to interruption. She added a troubled look and started talking to other tellers. Then she faced me and asked in English, "Where did you get this money?"

My mind flashed back to recent issues I had buying an international plane ticket. I couldn't use my bank card for it, so I had to transfer money to the travel company's bank account. I called them up and talked to the representative who gave me their account number. Call me paranoid, but then I called them again and spoke to another person just to make sure the first person didn't pull one over on me by giving me their own personal account number—that would've been a good one. What could I have done if I fell for a shenanigan like that? I'd be out over half-month's pay.

[On that note: What could I have done in the case of any offense against me? When in America, I assume a security blanket of knowing I can go to the courts. But in China, my ability to do this was greatly hindered. What could I have done if I had a work contract or pay issue? How about if a taxi driver drove off with my things in the car? I was grateful people were honest and good.]

When I was sure I got the right account number from the travel company, I went to my bank to transfer the funds. I thought this would be a cinch because the travel company happened to use the same bank as I. However, there was a chunk of paperwork and a nice fee on top of it anyway.

"I work here," I said to the teller. A helpful middle-aged lady in the line next to mine communicated to me that I needed to provide proof of employment. After all, how did they know I wasn't a...a...gosh, I don't know what they were fearing actually. Getting the proof they needed would have been difficult before my trip the next day. It dawned on me that all this waiting was for nothing. I left with those very same pink 100-yuan bills.

Running short on time, I considered a black-market alternative. Almost daily, I'd see middle-aged women (sometimes one, sometimes four or five) standing or sitting on a stool on a specific corner in my neighborhood. Once in a while I'd notice all the colorful bills in their front-facing fanny packs and eventually figured out they were money-changers. Perhaps this black market sprouted from the void that bank red tape secured.

The way they worked the corner with their black-market niche, they reminded me of prostitutes but didn't dress or look the part. I approached one and asked, *"Nǐ yǒu Hong Kong qián mǎ?"* ("Do you have Hong Kong money?" The word *ma* turns a statement into a yes/no question in Mandarin Chinese.) She indicated yes and showed me her fee via her calculator.

I came back later that day with my money, but further inquisition had me a little nervous. She was looking over my shoulder all the time as we talked. It felt like a drug deal, and before I extracted my money, I indicated my disinterest, thanked her, and walked away. If I had little to no recourse from banks and employers, I had absolutely none if she stiffed me. Speaking of being vulnerable, though, these ladies—unless they knew martial arts—were not in a position to defend themselves against thieves, yet they stood there with stacks and stacks of 100RMB and 100 Hong Kong Dollar notes. I bet they had 10,000RMB worth. In my neighborhood in Minneapolis I'd give them thirty-six hours before someone caught wind of their presence and robbed them.

I finally just decided to bring my Chinese money to Hong Kong and exchange it over there. Interestingly though, the solution to my money problem lay in the most convenient spot of all: inside the ferry port. And they even offered a good exchange rate.

***

Hong Kong: A Place Unlike Any Other

Hong Kong isn't just another city in China. Hong Kong is a landmark standing as a focus of economists, businesspeople, urban planners, technicians, and travelers and known for its opulence, world-famous skyline, public services, international population base, and of course, banking. Time and again while there, I felt as though I was in the center of it all. And it had me discerning and wondering about the ingredients making up this one-of-a-kind urban recipe that gets everyone's attention.

I first learned about Hong Kong as a child. I looked at the label on one of my awesome shirts: "Made in Hong Kong." I thought nothing of it except that this was a faraway, funny-sounding place populated by faraway, funny-sounding people. Twenty-some years later I can see the significance of that label. Why did it say Hong Kong instead of just China? And for that matter, why was I able to wear clothes from what was a then-isolated China anyway?

Like Macau, Hong Kong is both a city and a region—a Special Administrative Region (SAR). Also like Macau, Hong Kong was recently handed back to China as a former Western colony—from England in 1997, Macau from Portugal in 1999. This helped explain my shirt; when I was young, Hong Kong was literally a separate country. Today, it belongs to China but exists under that "One Country, Two Systems" policy, so it maintains a separate legal and social code, currency, immigration policy, police, etc. (This actually means that within a fifty-mile (80 km) area— Macau, Hong Kong, and the mainland—there is one country, *three* systems.) Customs to deal with and borders to cross? Sure. But the sovereignty of these little escapes meant some great variety down in southern Guangdong Province.

Hong Kong is much larger than Macau, but as far as nations go, it would rank among the smallest. As far as cities, it's a biggie—seven million. And it boasts one of the great skylines on earth.

(Wikipedia.org)

Here's where it lies in the Pearl River Delta region:

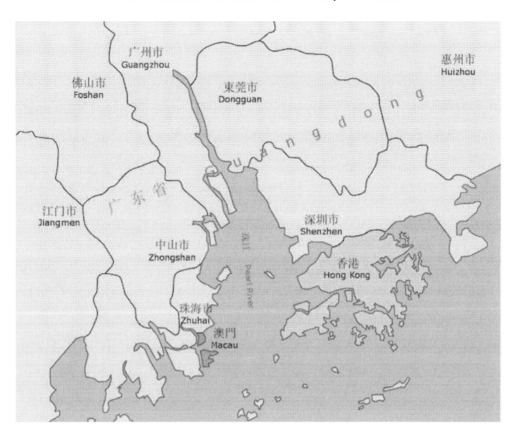

The British wrested control of this key port region following China's refusal to import opium in 1842 in what is now known appropriately as the Opium War. Yes, the British were warring to be *able* to sell drugs back then. China didn't want opium in their country, but that would harm British commerce, so England and the Chinese fought and the Crown won. China ceded Hong Kong Island to Britain in perpetuity—in other words, forever. And as a result of subsequent conflicts, additional area on the mainland was in Britain's hands, resulting in the region of Hong Kong we know today.

Dwarfed by its giant motherland, tiny Hong Kong existed independent from China throughout the 1900s. Its rise was in clear contrast to the mainland's poverty. Citizens from the mainland often tried to sneak into Hong Kong for the chance at a freer, more prosperous life. In fact, an adult student in one of my classes shared how her uncle swam from Zhuhai to Hong Kong on a banana tree. That's a long way. It took seventy minutes by high-speed ferry which I'm guessing went forty miles per hour (64kmh).

She shared in this class that he set off at night. I pictured him walking into the dark waters, laying down on his flotation device, and starting to kick. He endured hours of this with the eerie sea depth beneath and the stars and moonlight above. At some point during his faithful kicking, he spotted light up ahead. Others in this class corroborated her story by echoing the normalcy of this just a few decades ago. It's incredible what extremes people went/will/have to go to for a better life. It's incredible how far China has come in such a short amount of time. No one is swimming anymore.

When Britain ceded Hong Kong back to China in 1997, many were concerned what would happen. Britain had allowed it to thrive, and China had a less-flattering history of prosperity—especially toward that which was deemed "Western." Meanwhile, 150 years of British rule had indeed shaped economic and commercial presences, language, religion, and art. Thankfully, though, China has largely let Hong Kong be Hong Kong and even opened up financial doors in surrounding cities—like Zhuhai—so the contrast between the mainland and Hong Kong is much less drastic then it was even in the 90s. To put Hong Kong's prosperity into perspective, when it was handed back over to China, the population of the country increased by just a drop in the bucket. Yet this tiny region—426 sq mi (1,104 km²), which is smaller than the Twin Cities metro region—increased China's GDP by 25 percent.

I woke early on a mid-December morning to see Hong Kong for the first time. I hailed a taxi from my neighborhood to catch the ferry from the Zhuhai port.

It was like a small airport—ticket lines, expensive food, duty free items—except here it was a boatport.

Once through security, and my Hong Kong dollars in hand, I walked out and aboard a large vessel that held probably two hundred seated passengers on two levels: the haves and the not-so haves.

Being a not-so, I found a seat on the main level. Fittingly, they played some British-imported comedy—"Mr. Bean"—on the two televisions up front. I turned around and got a glimpse of my fellow passengers.

Mr. Bean did not amuse.

After an hour cruising on this cloudy day, I looked out one of the cabin windows to see the small, outlying islands of Hong Kong glide by. Though there are many islands, saying "Hong Kong Island" refers to the original settlement that is home to that incredible skyline.

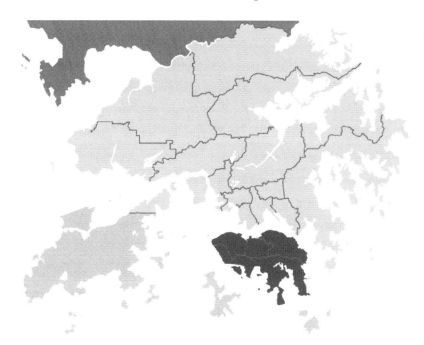

Hong Kong Special Administrative Region (SAR) is light grey. Hong Kong Island, our destination, is in dark green. (wikipedia.org)

Soon I could see the buildings of Hong Kong. Minutes later, the boat docked on the north side of the island, and we stood to go. I squeezed my way off the boat and through customs. After getting my passport stamped, I walked across the footbridge that stretched over the coastal street from the port to the city. I looked down below.

Hong Kong's red taxis under the bridge to the left and double-decker street cars deliver the dense population to their destinations

I took the stairs down the other side of the bridge to the street level and began my introduction. Hong Kong Island of the Hong Kong SAR reminded me of Manhattan Island of New York City. It's the heartbeat—specifically its district known as Central, which was where the port was.

Skyscrapers tunneled me in as I walked Hong Kong's busy, clean streets past newsstands, food vendors, and other pedestrians.

I like how the downtown of a big city can give you that in-between feeling of being outdoors yet still sheltered.

Of the thirty tallest buildings in the world, Hong Kong's monuments of banking and business include four.

My trusty guidebook recommended a "45-minute" walking tour of Central taking me through the sharp snazz of Hong Kong but also an elegant plaza, relaxing park, and a church snuggled into this dense district. Starting off, it was hard to miss some of these "Four Tallest."

Across the channel in the Kowloon district

Right here in Central at the walking tour's starting point

Soon the attractions had me looking back at the ground.

Statue of the HSBC banker, Sir Thomas Jackson, facing the Legislative Council Building in the plaza, Statue Square

Further along, other artsy urban areas appeared with fountains shooting out of shallow pools in the center of open, clean walkways surrounded by flowers, lawns, and trees. I continued away from the skyscrapers and toward a large park.

The buildings in the background made for a tasty contrast of urban and nature.

Through this park and circling back toward the starting point of my tour, I was directed behind the skyscrapers. Nestled back here was an old building from the British colonial days.

An Anglican church

I had yet to see a church on the mainland, so it was the first I'd seen in months. I crept inside to find an unlit and almost totally silent sanctuary with a few people scattered in the pews saying their prayers.

Whether a cathedral in Minneapolis or this church in Hong Kong, the rich silence of a house of worship is universal, a palpable mass emanating from the penetrating imagery and from the worship and meditation of those within this large, echoing, open space.

After soaking in some stillness, I walked back outside and across the stone surface of the church grounds to the church bookstore. I had a few words with an Indian female clerk, who happily stated that the church in Hong Kong was strong and growing. From what I heard, Christianity on the mainland was growing, too. There, churches are legal, but require state permission. There was one in Zhuhai that I regretfully never visited. A fellow English teacher—and elderly Englishman—did, however, and told me it was full each week.

My walking tour then circled me back to another of these "tallest four".

Bank of China Building

And I wrapped up this ~~45 minute~~ three-hour tour by enjoying perhaps the most iconic symbols of Hong Kong: the lion statues outside the Hong Kong and Shanghai Bank Corporation (HSBC) Building. These guys have been guarding this building entrance for decades, even sporting bullet grazes on them from World War Two when the Japanese invaded and occupied this island.

As representatives of the swaths of wealth generated and moving through this city, Hong Kong puts this mascot on their currency.

Right on the money

Hong Kong's prosperity was evident this entire tour. It showed up in the parks and buildings; it showed up on the streets as seen by the cars.

It showed up along the streets.

Western holiday décor

And it showed up in its retail.

After saying goodbye to the lions, I spotted a branch store of the designer brand, Louis Vuitton. In China, Louis Vuitton (LV) was a big deal. I had heard students of mine—young and old—joke about being rich and indicate "LV" as *the* brand of wealth. There also wasn't a more knocked-off brand sold on the streets of Zhuhai. To me, the interest in designer brands goes right by me like people's interest in a sport I don't follow. It was precisely because of this un-relating, though—enhanced by being a foreigner and as someone without nearly the needed number of nills in my bank account to buy anything—that I had to check out this store.

The space inside was warmly lit, filling a room of metal-accented woodwork. Handbags were displayed on their own individual wall spaces, and jackets deserving of their own hanger display were featured in the center. Billfolds and jewelry rested behind a glass counter. With LV, though, it's all about the bags. The cheaper ones were $13,500.

Relax. That's in Hong Kong dollars. In American, it's a measly two grand.

The salespeople in their black business attire and matching clean, black haircuts clashed with the loose T-shirts, messy hair, and unshaven faces of the street salespeople. The customers here, naturally, also clashed with the street shoppers. I watched Chinese women examining the goods behind the glass, pointing out a piece, and then the salesperson handing it to them for a closer look. I thought it odd that they weren't deterred by prices. And it wasn't just one or two wealthy people within, but a population comparable to any busy store back in the United States during the Christmas season. It brought to light just how many rich folks are out there shopping, eating out, driving cars, and living a life that hovers a few pay scales above most others.

However, I also found it odd because even if I was rich, I would have thought that the need to be modern and stylish would hit a breaking point when the amount spent far exceeds any increase in utility. I thought it would have been fitting for one shopper to stop when realizing what they were doing, turn to another, and say, "You know, we can get a purse 98 percent cheaper somewhere else."

I learned not to underestimate the effect one's world—one's social/cultural bubble—has on one's overall perspective and perception. These shoppers looked as caught up in their own trend-chasing lives as anyone else—indeed, as I had been while choosing a wristwatch from Sears. (And I now have two wristwatches. Aren't I a materialistic schmuck when compared to the man who has none?) At the upper financial end, though, such materialism is easier to recognize, and thus, judge. They spend $2,000 on what costs $20 at Wal-Mart—Wal-Mart being, of course, too expensive for many people living in China.

I suppose it feels good, perhaps comforting, to make a purchase and possess a brand people associate with glamour. Presumably, the gentleman seen here would make some lady a happy camper come Christmas:

"$2,000, huh? Say, does that include gift-wrapping?"

I asked the worker in the picture above if the phones ring a lot when a new line of bags come out—like how other consumers might eagerly await a new cell phone or tennis shoe. She said they do.

This evening, I met my friend, Dennis, who was here on business. We went out for dinner on Lan Kwai Fong, a street lined with bars and clubs that Western tourists and Western Hong Kong residents flock to at night.

Looking down on Lan Kwai Fong

We talked over dinner about his business and about Hong Kong. Born in Vietnam, Dennis, age forty, came to America when he was five. He graduated college and went on to attain his MBA and law degree, afterwards working for an investment bank in New York. From New York he went out on his own and back out East to Shanghai and then right here in Hong Kong to start New Asia Partners, a private equity investment firm. Basically, he takes investors' dollars and puts them into Asian companies to help them go public. (I'm still curious how one would make their first deal or get their first investor or find a company to help go public; but it's what he did, and now he owns a nice, big home on a lake.) Dennis lived out here for nine years before heading back to America and settling down in Minneapolis, where he continues to run his company.

Dennis's take on Hong Kong is a popular one among fiscally conservative people and provides insight into what makes Hong Kong successful. Dennis lauded the free-market ways of Hong Kong. Its tax rate is a flat 15 percent for individuals and either 15 or 16.5 percent for businesses. There is no capital gains tax. There is no estate tax. There is no sales tax. Yet at the same time, the government can offer terrific education, public transportation, and health care which Progressives would applaud. According to Wikipedia, "Hong Kong is one of the healthiest places in the world." I experienced the public transit for myself.

Earlier this day, I entered the subway infrastructure and found each aspect—stairs/escalators, hallways, and platform—to be clean and modern. You actually couldn't see the tracks. They were sealed off by a glass wall with sliding doors lining up with the sliding subway car doors when it was time to board.

I recalled New York City and asked, "Where are the rats?"

I boarded my train. During the ride I heard and felt only the hum of the car gliding through the tunnel and a clear, female voice informing us about upcoming stops. I felt as if I was in a simulator of "What the year 2020 is going to be like." I wondered how Hong Kong seems to have its cake and eat it too: low taxes, nicer public offerings. New York is wealthier. New York has higher taxes. New York isn't as nice.

We all have observable ideas and a moral compass telling us what makes an effective society tick. But given the random recipe of ingredients here—British Law and policy, the region's Chinese citizens, a good harbor location, timing—I don't think anyone could've predicted that such factors would have led to such a clean, prosperous place. And there's the chicken-and-egg debate: Was the policy here as the result, or the creator, of the situation?

Unfortunately, I only had the one day and night here before my need to return the following morning. Dennis and I grabbed breakfast, and I went back to the ferry port on the north end of Central to ride back to Zhuhai.

***

Chapter Nine: Happy Holidays

When I moved to China I figured I'd miss out on celebrating some of my usual holidays. So just as when I saw Halloween décor, I was pleasantly surprised to see this sign of Christmas:

Outside a grocery store in Zhuhai

I also found a Santa hat for 3RMB (less than fifty cents) at a stationery store in my neighborhood. It was a hit with my young students. It was a hit with my adult ones, too. The night I wore my pointy, red hat with white fuzz ball atop, my second quarter adult class asked me about it.

"It's...uh...a Santa hat," I said not knowing what to call it.

When teaching English, I'd hear questions about my language I hadn't considered before. "Gosh, I don't know why we use articles," I'd think to myself. "I thought everyone did." It was an education in something I never "learned" because I just grew up with it. The same thing happened with Santa Claus. As I told these adults about him living in the North Pole with his sleigh pulled by flying reindeer, I realized how odd the story sounded.

In turn, I asked them about how they celebrate Christmas. Most of these eight or nine adults said they do buy a gift for someone. However, about six of them thirty years and older shared that this was a new tradition for them. None of them as children recognized—or even knew about—Christmas. But as the new millennium came, they slowly started to recognize the holiday in their own, secular way. And now, at least in urban centers, Christmas has quite a presence.

Regardless of any recognition, I had to teach Christmas Day. I arrived Saturday, December 25, trying to ignore this fact; it wasn't too hard because here it wasn't considered an odd day to work. My first class of six-year-olds came and went like any other day. My second class, though, rekindled my Christmas spirit when a couple eight-year-old girls gave me their handmade cards pictured here:

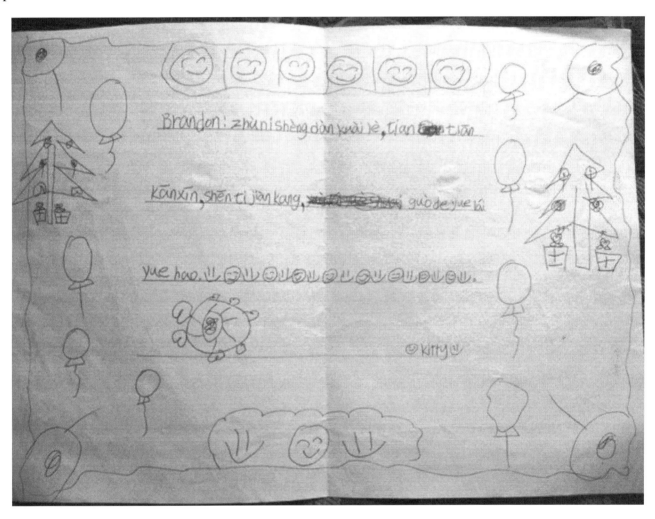

This being my first teaching job, my heart warmed with the first-time reception of a student's gift. This was especially so because I was far from home during my favorite holiday and simultaneously reminded—through their gifts—the reason this holiday is my favorite. It was a pleasantly surprising Merry Christmas, er, I mean Happy Christmas.

Window at my school

For my family back home, I sent a large box and watched them open their gifts via Skype. Though I could negotiate my Christmas bill significantly at The Underground Market, I unfortunately couldn't do so with the lady at the post office who charged as much to send the box of goods (and it took a month) as it did to buy all the gifts. But it arrived in time and watching my brothers, sister, parents, and grandparents check out their gifts—zodiac wall clock, oversized China nature-themed wall calendars, jewelry, silk scarf, and a couple toys for the nephews—was a unique and memorable holiday connection with loved ones.

One week later came the New Year—*Western* New Year, that is, which China celebrates as they are on the Western calendar. So on December 31, I went out with some students to one of the two Western bars in town. The guys drank beers.

And the gals had hot tea.

At midnight, a bunch of middle-aged English and Irish expats rang things in right. With confetti falling and Auld Lang Syne blaring, they cheered and hugged one another in a euphoric celebration of life.

***

Chinese New Year Celebration

Any Western New Year celebration was just a warm-up. The real deal was the Chinese New Year, a celebration and break lasting two to three weeks and the impetus for the largest human migration on Earth: Chinese migrant workers return home to be with family. Chinese New Year moves around from the end of January to early/mid February in accordance with the lunar calendar. Each annual cycle signifies the changing of the Chinese zodiac animal. 2011 would be that of the Rabbit.

TPR hopped into the New Year with style, having the means, the size, and the venue to hold their own celebration. Along with school branches, Simone had also acquired an old temple property in western Zhuhai. Built between the late-1700s and mid-1800s, what is now known as The Beishan East-West Cultural Hub was once the former Beishan Village town center, a complex of three individual temples, meeting hall, and theater for the then-village twenty minutes west of Gongbei. These buildings serve as standing time capsules of China a century and a half ago.

Outside one of the temple buildings. They were grey-bricked with clay-shingled roofs.

TPR renovated the property to include a large theater, meeting room, an exhibit of artifacts, and exterior aspects such as the plaza and walkways. The vision was to use it for concerts, business conventions...and New Year's celebrations. And more than just ringing in the New Year, TPR's New Year's celebration served as an annual recognition of the school's accomplishments and standout employees. With the mixed-language audience of about 250, they were in need of two emcees. TPR asked me to be the English one.

I arrived at the Beishan theater early afternoon on January 25. This gave me some time to wait around the historic, solid, but drafty structure until the celebration that evening. With no heat, and refrigerator-like conditions outside, I paced around trying to stay warm while watching the crew, decorators, and organizers prepare. I guess I took the role of the spoiled talent and asked for a sweater, a blanket, anything. Shame on my Minnesotan self.

[Let me take this opportunity to mention the heating of buildings—most weren't. This isn't a problem for ten of the twelve months of the year here in southern China. But for these other two, there was rarely escaping the sub-50 F (sub-10 C) degree temperatures. I didn't know how cold that could feel until I had to wake up in it, shower in it, teach in it, shop in it...

I bought a space heater for my bedroom, but I couldn't escape the cold anywhere else in my apartment. This includes the shower as the trickle of its reliably-weak pressure wasn't enough to prevent my shivering or even keep my arm hair from sticking straight out. Jusco was heated. So I showered at my gym and spent many heavenly minutes in their steam room. Outside of this, though, it was all chilly. Students wore their winter coats in class; I taught in my winter gear. One benefit was that I never needed an eraser for the white board as my gloves worked just fine for deleting mistakes.

The cold got to me more than to the locals. To them it was normal. None of my adult students in that second quarter class even had space heaters in their homes. They just wore a lot of layers, they said. They were hearty. And frankly, we were fortunate to be in the climate of the southern coast. Later in the year I met a thirty-something English teacher from the American Midwest who shared with me his trials teaching in a city a couple provinces north of me. No heat there, either. Apparently there's some unwritten rule that cities south of Shanghai go without heat.

"Doesn't it snow there?" I asked him with some incredulity.

"Oh yeah," he responded with some animation.]

Eventually, though, things started to heat up backstage in the theater with the energy of show time.

My school dressed me in black slacks and a fitted deep red jacket fastened with black rope-loop buttons and a yellow dragon insignia along my right shoulder. My co-host, whom I had met an hour before showtime, was a fortyish, smaller-statured, friendly-looking Chinese gentlemen all decked out in a long-tailed tux. He would lead the show while I kept the English-speaking audience in the know.

After I was all ready, I peeked out from backstage to see people filling the seats and awaiting the start of the show with expectant chatter. Things were getting real. A couple minutes later the houselights dimmed, the spotlight shone, and the curtains drew back. From my perch offstage right, I watched the tuxedoed Chinese host walk out to the applause of an eager audience and animatedly welcome the crowd using voice, face, and arms. In the shadows, I listened to his bright confidence and the audience's approving laughter. Five months prior, I was brand new to China, dressed down, and nervous to get out there to dance. This time I was acquainted with many members of the audience, dressed in a sleek getup, and nervous to get out there and speak.

I rehearsed the notes I had written to introduce myself and transition between awards and performances. I even had some phrases in Chinese to warm myself to the crowd. It was hard to concentrate on my Mandarin, though. I feared stepping out into the light and interrupting what sounded like a successful opening by my talented and experienced co-host. I realized the importance of making a good entrance. If my nerves took over right away, they'd run the show, and it would be a long night. So, I imagined I could best face and expel my nervous energy by sprinting out onstage. I once saw a taping of David Letterman, and in his pre-show audience warm-up he came running out to the audience's delight.

But I changed my mind, thinking instead to walk out there as if I didn't know where I was, as in thinking, "What am I doing here in this outfit in front of all these people?" It was an act—but it also wasn't. I don't remember how I even knew when to go. I think there was a producer backstage to prompt me. Whatever cue alerted me, I put away my notes and walked out.

I couldn't see most of the audience with the bright stage lights pointed at me, but I felt their gaze.

[It's funny how we go through life wanting a certain amount of attention—no one wants to be completely ignored. The approval of others is nourishing and builds us up. But then when in the spotlight, we assume responsibility for others' contentment which can cripple; like their eyes are draining our certainty, confidence, and freedom to be us.]

Whatever. I went with my schtick.

I wandered out looking around and then asked in Chinese where I was. Maybe it was my poor Mandarin, maybe my bad acting, maybe it wasn't terribly funny, but the audience only offered so-so laughter. Then I asked in Mandarin if I was dreaming. The audience again chuckled, and this time the co-host added some banter to play along. After his few sentences, ending in an exclamation, the audience welcomed me with some cheer.

Next, I took out my notes and spoke more Mandarin: "Good evening!" and "I'm glad to be your host." They appreciated these attempts with louder applause and the night got underway.

Not only was this event for TPR, it was mainly by TPR. One young woman office worker did a Lady Gaga lip-sync dance routine, another group of women performed a line dance to the song "Jambalaya (On the Bayou)", and one young gentlemen rapped an Eminem song. Awards were handed out for Teacher of the Year, Administrator of the Year, and Employee of the Year. We drew tickets for prizes such as cash, a designer watch, and a bicycle—which I pedaled down the aisle from the rear of the theater to the surprise of attendees.

My co-host and I traded talk time, his segues and introductions going first followed by my own. It's too bad we couldn't communicate. Chemistry was hard to come by. Then again, maybe that made for better entertainment.

I had been observing China all year. It was interesting to be the one watched—to observe those observing me—during this most significant of cultural events.

Xin Nian Kuai le!

***

The New Year's celebration marked the halfway point of my year in China. Over the long break, I migrated—escaping the cool weather, crowded buses, and the routine of working in China for an exploratory fifteen days of warmth and wander in Vietnam and Cambodia. I returned to China mid-February.

Chapter Ten: Welcome Home

It was now the Year of the Rabbit in China. At home, my flatmate Heath jackrabbitted out of here, taking his savings and planning to motorcycle the length of Vietnam. A new teacher took his room, a low-key forty-year-old German-American named Kurt.

I was refreshed and ready to get back to work. But like the fall, even before I had a chance to step foot into a classroom, my school wanted me to perform in a community celebration. So upon returning, things picked up right where they left off—in costume.

For the Lantern Festival parade, celebrated on the last day of the Chinese New Year, TPR staff was asked to walk.

By wearing something a little more appropriate for a Chinese celebration, I felt like I got a little redemption for my clash of a dance routine at the community celebration in the fall. John, the mustached sixty-year-old teacher from upstate New York who also was on stage in the fall, got his own redo by taking things in the opposite direction and wearing a conspicuously American look—a cowboy—a look never more obvious than while worn in China. You can see him in the picture on the left, as well.

But despite what we wore, we stuck out. And when we approached the hoards of onlookers alongside the parade route, even after our candy long since ran out, people were eager just to have us come near them. As expected, the children were excited to have me come by and say hello; surprisingly, the mothers were also eager to reach out and shake our hands. But I was most impressed by how several men reacted—grown men whose faces lit up when I simply looked at them and waved. I felt like a celebrity. The newspaper the following Sunday helped cement the fantasy:

Throughout the year, I must have had seventy-five little kids walk by and say to me real loud, "Hello!" I was also asked occasionally by adults if I was American—not Russian or Canadian or German or English or Australian. Such interactions (usually with a twenty- to thirty-year-old man or woman) sometimes ended by us exchanging numbers with the hope of starting a friendship. On one occasion I met some curious college-aged spectators on the sidewalks of Zhuhai, whom I got to know and with whom I later shared a game of ping-pong back at my apartment.

They were without English names and wanted them. I was honored to dub them Luther, Edward, Howard, and Libby. It was a simple, though rich, experience. I just looked into their eyes and saw what came to mind. It made me think I ought to wait to name my future children until the day they are born.

Naming went both ways. I became known as *Fēng Xiáng* (烽 翔) courtesy of my adult student, Emily—the hill-climbing accountant. I modified it a little bit. *Feng* (which in Chinese would be the surname—as in, call me Mr. Feng) means many things, especially when not distinguished with a tone. Besides being a common surname in Chinese, *feng's* (冯) most common attribution in Mandarin is *fēng* (风) which means "wind." I looked at all the fengs and found one more appropriate for me—the character I wrote above—which means "beacon fire." I chose it because my name, Brandon, is said to have origins in the same meaning. *Xiang* I left as Emily gave it to me; it means "soar" or "glide." I've since been told by Chinese people that it's an unorthodox name. Oh well. I would find out later this year that after just a couple days being called only Fēng Xiáng, you get used to being called a new name pretty quickly—as if it's been yours all along. And nothing would make me feel more at home in this country.

***

Back in the Swing of Things

Teaching kicked off again, and with even just a semester under my belt, I felt a lot more comfortable. I'd teach the same curriculum to the same ages at the same branches. Saturdays and Sundays were once again packed with young students and my weekdays were for my adult classes. One change was that TPR had me work with a couple teenagers one-on-one.

One student was a fifteen-year-old girl whose mother happened to inquire about TPR's tutoring services at their headquarters when I was standing in the lobby. She explained that her daughter was moving to Singapore in only eight weeks time to attend an English-speaking school. I offered to help by devising a curriculum of academic English. I could imagine her daughter's challenges given the discrepancy between being conversational in a language and knowing scholastic lingo. Her mom accepted, and I started meeting with Jacqueline—a tall, shy teenager with hip glasses, short haircut, and a penchant for the Twilight vampire books. Twice a week we met at the Jida branch to learn both general English according to a textbook curriculum and then a particular subject lingo. One week was literature and included such applicable words as *fiction, poetry, verse,* and *narrator.* The next week was math and we focused on words that included *sphere, exponent, average,* and *decimal.* Finally we studied the sciences, such as chemistry and biology, and their respective terminologies.

I also got to work with a twelve-year-old named Michael, a boy with the body of a man and the golf swing of a champ. We worked together for four months on general English at the headquarters branch in my neighborhood. Besides the cheesy songs—"This and That at the Laundromat"—and the written dialogue and grammar exercises, we took to the street to apply lessons in prepositions: "The bakery is **next to** the restaurant." Michael was himself prepping for an English-speaking school the following year in Macau, but at his age and ability, he needed to work on a better foundation of the language.

Michael and I would hang out once in a while outside of class. His parents—both were very tall and athletic—owned an athletic club in Zhuhai, and one afternoon Michael took me to the club's driving range. On another occasion, his parents treated us to a round of golf at Zhuhai's nicest country club.

The health club and golf course were interesting to experience; the chance for Michael to use English in settings outside of school was great for his proficiency.

Indeed, both Michael and Jacqueline went to their respective English schools and did well.

My third adult class of the year was a hodgepodge of young/middle-aged, professional/blue-collar, urban/rural-raised individuals. Unlike how I described my children students earlier, some of these young adults were quite stoic and inhibited in expression.

I was teaching this class one night in March when the subject of family came up. While writing on the white board, I specifically asked if any pupils had any living grandparents. A twenty-six-year-old named June affirmed she had, adding the detail that her grandmother was ninety-nine. I stopped writing.

"June, does she have the little feet?," I asked.

"Yes."

"Can I visit her?"

A bewildered June semi-smiled in laughing agreement as she explained that her grandmother lived a long ways from Zhuhai. That was fine with me. Soon after arriving to China, I learned that some elderly women still lived with the bound feet of ancient times. I wanted to meet one of these living legends, that hearkened to a totally different China than the one I lived in. So when June shared that in class, I mentally penciled in her grandmother as a stop on a trek through central China I was planning for the summer. I then got back to reviewing such words as *cousin, nephew, niece, aunt,* and *uncle* which were oftentimes as useless as *brother* and *sister* in one-child China.

***

June's grandmother interested me because of the division in China she represented between now and yesteryear. The experiences described in this next chapter all contributed to my understanding of the diversity to be had in China today. Within them were also themes such as migrant employment and, as exemplified in the following journey, the power of nature.

Chapter Eleven: Two Chinas

Yangshuo

There are many possible visions that come to mind when one hears the word "China": The Great Wall, a horizon of drab apartment high-rises, crowded city streets. How about dramatic, jagged terrain jutting through and shaping the banks of gorgeous rivers?

Now we're talking.

Yangshuo is a small city located in Guangxi, the province next door to mine. Throughout the year, I had heard other Westerners speak of Yangshuo as a great place to visit. I had also been teased all year by an image of its scenery on the 20-yuan note.

A picture is worth a thousand words...and about three bucks.

So over a long holiday weekend in early April—the Qing Ming Festival (*Qīng míng Jié*, 清明节), which is Ancestor's Day or Tomb Sweeping Day—my Chinese friend Lucy, my American friend Reynold, and I took to the road in Lucy's VW Beetle for this gotta-see-it-with-your-own-eyes destination.

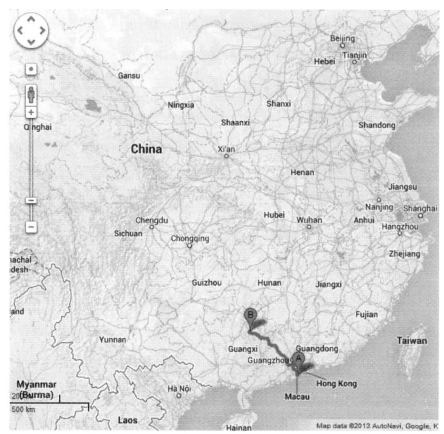

It's a short way on the map, but still an eight hour drive. And on the way, the lesson of this chapter surfaced on the terrain we drove to see.

We started off from the hilly, urbanized coast of Zhuhai, past the flatter earth around Guangzhou, and back into some up-and-down terrain of inner Guangdong Province. Here, we passed through smaller cities.

The further inland we got, the more desolate things became. Nearing the border of Guangxi, we spotted a mountain village.

...with mountain folk...

...enjoying mountain lifestyles.

This village reminded me of the notion Lucy brought up to me way back in the fall. We first met while dining with mutual friends on a restaurant patio along the Zhuhai coast. A friend of Reynold, Lucy had soft, straight, shoulder-length hair and a light complexion. She worked in management for a manufacturer and while we ate on the patio, told me I hadn't yet seen "real" China. There are two Chinas to discover, she added. The Starbucks, shiny silverware, and shopping malls of Zhuhai weren't the whole story.

By the time we took this trip, I had realized this in some respects. I had seen all year within Zhuhai the wealthy BMW drivers versus poor people on shoddy bikes. Here in this mountain town, though, was a new "Two China" wrinkle: the developed urban life we left behind versus this more traditional lifestyle of rural China. It seemed the people here still lived with luxuries such as vehicles and electronics, but nonetheless maintained a slower, quieter existence closer to nature and minus the frills. It was analogous to, but more exaggerated than, my life growing up in Blackduck, Minnesota, when it was compared to United States city life.

We didn't stay long, and soon after driving off from this town, encountered a much starker "Two China" example: the ethnic divide.

There is more to the Chinese people than what we Americans are regularly exposed to. The ethnicity we picture when hearing "China"—the Han—do make up 93 percent of China's population. They include everyone from Jackie Chan to Yao Ming to all the political figures we see and hear about. Making up the other 7 percent are groups such as the Tibetans of western China, the Uighurs of northwest China, and the Manchus—as in "The Manchurian Candidate"—in the northeast. But there are fifty-two other officially-recognized populations in China—all with their own language and customs. Thus, this "Two China" split actually breaks into fifty-six.

Driving around a bend in the increasingly rugged terrain crossing into Guangxi province, we met three women walking down the center of the road leading a small herd of water buffalo. The three middle-aged women wore stockings over their dark pants. On top they had dark-blue robes with light blue edges, and their hair was done up with white scarves. We slowed—not just because we wanted to stop, but because we had no other choice.

"Our way or the highway."

I got out and followed these beasts clip-clopping along the blacktop in the middle of their village. Two of the women then guided the giants off to the right, behind brick homes, and into a watering hole.

He never did take it.

I'd later learn that these women were from the Zhuang people (Zhuàng zú, 壮族, or, in the Zhuang language, Bouxcuengh).

Their population in China, estimated at eighteen million, puts the Zhuang second only to the Han majority's nine hundred million. So though a distant second, they are the largest minority in China. Here's a map of the ethnic distribution throughout China:

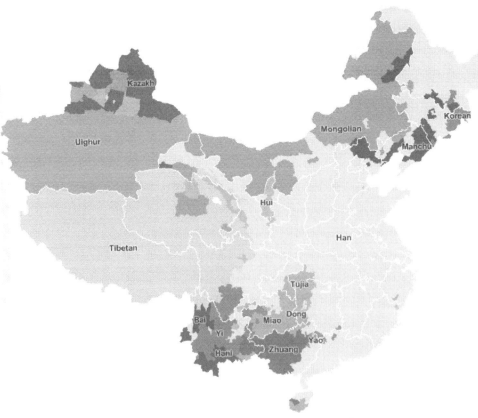

Within these fifteen are fifty-five subsets.

I bid the Zhuang women farewell and walked back to the car. On that smooth, newly-layered blacktop slicing down the middle of this village, traffic cruises by at forty-five miles per hour, passing the Zhuang living life at ten miles per hour. Out here, though, it was the pavement and vehicles that stuck out in a backdrop of livestock, small farms, and people with handmade clothes. These sorts of "Two China" intersections continue in countless forms all over the country as development encroaches and cultures mingle/clash. I just hope the best of each is allowed to thrive in the process.

Soon after we left the village the skies began to darken. Looking out from the back seat of Lucy's car, I caught glimpses of mountainous monster silhouettes silently standing within the black rural of Guangxi. (Mountainous terrain might typically be imagined as triangular hills, but Yangshuo is different. The topography is considered "karst": limestone worn away over the years leaving jagged, cavernous terrain. In the case of Yangshou, the landscape is lined with giant pillars.) I liked not seeing much around in the darkness. It made the scenery a bit of a mystery and all the more surprising when seeing it the following day. We pulled into Yangshuo at 9:00 p.m., found our hostel, and settled in for the night.

Earth's Teeth

Nine hours later I awoke in a room with five Europeans—all of us in three bunk beds. I quietly got dressed in a couple layers for the cool highlands and left my lodging that was tucked away in the back alleys of Yangshuo. The narrow corridors were damp and drab—but not "city" drab. The stone and brick and concrete making up these outdoor hallways felt earthy and refreshing, as if these manmade structures were inspired by the land around it. The alleys eventually opened onto a street.

Along pedestrian-only West Street, most establishments hadn't opened yet.

The air was crisp and cool, cloudy but not wet. The area encompassed a common vibe of China—not paradise, but a place of history and genuineness (even in this touristy location).

The surrounding geology made the municipality feel nestled within the arms of nature's alleys. I anticipated the beauty of these monoliths in the countryside and had just two full days to take in the surreal scenery. I'd spend each day along—or on—one of its two main rivers: the Li and the Yulong.

The Li, the widest river, is on the right; the Yulong, the second widest, is along the left side. This first day I'd explore the Li.

I walked the length of West Street where, at its perpendicular meeting point with a main road, was a bus station parking lot. I found and hopped aboard the shuttle taking me and a busload of Chinese tourists north to the drop-off upriver on the Li. From there, my plan was to take a boat ride six miles south and then go by foot the remaining four to the town of Xing Ping where I'd take a shuttle back to Yangshuo.

At our drop-off upriver, busloads of people became boatloads.

Pictured below is where the scenery started off with a bang—or better yet, a ka-ching:

There's the money shot. Look familiar?

I saw several tourists stand and pose with bill in hand.

It seemed a paper currency pilgrimage or at least a nifty item to cross off the ol' bucket list.

Down over the edge were the vehicles for our tour.

I walked down preparing for a more intimate view and interaction with this scenery. I walked aboard a flatboat and found they were steady, though you could still feel your weight manipulate its position in the water. I sat on one of the wood benches and awaited the ride down nature's highway and a river's-eye view of the magnificence it wove around.

Sitting there a few moments, though, cool air interrupted the warm energy of anticipation, and the accompanying wind produced along this river-plain gave me the chills. A shiver countered the comforting awe I was hoping for on this ride. Further thwarting my ideas of a peaceful journey, the captain started the chugging engine, adding an audial jolt to this uneasiness.

With just one other young passenger aboard, whose English name was London, we started along with a whole convoy of loud boats making the same journey. Though sturdy, the flatboat bumped from even these modest river waves—adding another restless element to the chilly, noisy ride. Then, one final sensory element was the cherry on top. And this one I can't say I didn't ask for, because if it was intimacy with the river I wanted, I got it in the form of chilly pieces of it splashing up and dotting my face, chest, and shirtsleeves. In all, it was cold, wet, bumpy, and noisy experience. All this stimulation to absorb, and I haven't even reached the most obvious sense.

Just as the darkness of the night before made the silhouettes of mountain pillars look like monsters, the weather and transportation through these lands transformed their appearance in the tint of its affect. On my VW car ride out to Yangshuo, I anticipated breath-taking wonder. What I got in this physically and audibly stimulating setting was the perception of abrasion, the peaks now resembling earth's teeth and the land meeting violently with the sky.

I learned an interesting truth at Yangshuo: such a dramatic environment doesn't necessarily yield the positive, moving experience that I expected when viewing photographs of this place in the comfort of my home. These peaks are also a catalyst, magnifying whichever emotional trajectory I happened to embody.

After a few more miles, we skidded onto a gradual bank. I stepped off the uncertain boat to plant my feet onto solid earth.

A rug of relaxing rocks. Suddenly my emotional trajectory was altered in an opposite, calming direction, magnified by this poetic, visual contrast to the gouging scenery about me.

It didn't take long for me to warm up after escaping the river sprinkle and wind—especially when someone there was selling hot tea. There were several vendors situated along a row of tables selling food and drinks to the few dozen tourists. Some vendors were out of the loop doing their own thing.

This man sold rocks that he found and sanded into smooth shape.

Man and nature in artistic union

Also here amongst the gathering was the union of man and animate nature.

The animate cormorant—which people here use for a very handy fishing technique.

With a rope around one of their ankles and a snare around their neck, these trained bird brains dive for fish like they were born to do, but return the fish to their handlers. The throat snare allows smaller fish to be eaten and the larger ones to be coughed up for the human above. Some guys have a whole crew out for the catch.

Past the rocky river edge was a large flat of dirt and patchy grass leading up to the the start of the hiking trail. Warm and reenergized, I collected my sightseeing senses for further on-foot exploration. I followed the south-flowing river with it to my right—sometimes near its edge, sometimes one hundred yards from the water. Soon after starting out, the footpath borrowed a local road for its route.

Along it I got to enjoy some personal interaction.

This boy bounced out of one of the roadside residences.

Then up ahead I saw an old man leading two buffalo to their pen.

I moseyed up to him, curious about the ways of life echoed off these peaks. He seemed happy I did so.

He also chuckled when his bull shrugged and huffed as I tried to pet it. It scared me. Those things are huge.

He then waved a cupped hand toward himself to indicate me to come inside his home.

I thought, "Hmmm, alright."

He led me up some steps to his roof while making a drinking motion with his hand to his mouth.

I followed him up the concrete steps and stood on the flat top of his home, taking in the elevated views of the countryside it afforded. I turned back toward the man, but all he did was walk back down the steps. Alone, I waited a little while—figured I'd enjoy the view some more. From the crowded, noisy, horn-honking ways of Zhuhai, Yangshuo was a refreshing panorama of picturesque, jigsaw puzzle-worthy scenery. He never returned. So I simply made my way back down the stairs and continued on my walk.

Soon, I saw more locals living their lives amongst the mountains.

Can you spot the old woman gardening?

Heckuva backyard

When locals weren't around, I simply enjoyed the way the scenery made me feel.

The quiet allowed me to hear each gravel crunch beneath my step.

As it did on the boat ride, the terrain magnified my emotions. Unlike the ride, however, the mountains now stood as comforting complements for the life that sprung from their floor.

Orange grove

The mountains also elicited the somber calm of life departed.

Afterwards was the home stretch of the hike.

In a union of local interaction and the power of the scenery, I saw this couple use the Li to demonstrate their own sentimental union:

Finally, the end of the hike treated me to one last view:

At the landing in the town, Xing Ping. From here, I took a shuttle back to Yangshuo.

The boat ride and hike on Day One turned up the volume on a breadth of emotions; Day Two would dig a little deeper.

Grateful for Rain

Normally I'd wish for blue skies like the next guy, but something about this place made the rain this next day feel appropriate. In fact, sunny weather would've been lacking.

Thank goodness I brought my raincoat, because visiting Yangshuo is all about being outdoors, and if rain comes, so be it. I exited those narrow alleys my second early morning to a wet West Street.

What do you do on a rainy day? How about rent a bike?

I had seen the bike rental place just off West Street the night I arrived. I returned to see a few old single-speed models standing out front of the small building. I was the only customer at the time. I picked out the best of the bunch, hopped atop the plain bicycle, and pedaled along the town roads, squinting my eyes in the sprinkle. The Yulong River west of town was my destination this day.

Businesses in town were opening, pedestrians were out with umbrellas, and cars joined me on the roads. It was just a drizzle outside, but it was still a drizzle. And with my hood wrapped over my head, it was all I could do to be cautious in the activity of even early morning small city Chinese traffic.

I was on a main street heading out of town but wanted to explore more of Yangshuo on this quiet Sunday morning, so I veered off onto a side road where traffic was nil and the town felt closer. Blocks of buildings now made way for a couple hills interrupting the middle of town. This break in urban action went well with the sprinkle. And one hill I glided by had a trail to the top. I hopped off my bike, secured it on the nearby bike rack, and made my way up the steps.

At the top, a dirt-floor clearing the size of a living room allowed the onlooker to stand and take in the view.

This grand view centered me by saying, "See? This is how small you are. Stop taking yourself so seriously."

A light breeze teamed with the expanse before me and the silence about me. I had that feeling you get from a slow walk in the woods or floating down a creek in a canoe all by yourself. But it was more than just the emotional sensation. The rain added to the effect (and affect) with a physical accompaniment. If I could combine calm and awe—"cawlm"—that's what I'd call it. And this inspired-by-nature feeling gave me the space to emote.

Standing there, I relaxed and let my guard down. Then, to my surprise, some nervousness and fear emerged, apparently needing this window to pass through. Then a thought attached to the feeling: the name of an old friend. I had forgotten his last name for years and had wanted to reconnect to apologize for something I did ten years prior in college. I had no obvious trigger to be thinking of this person; I hadn't been pondering his name or recalling the instance from which to be thinking of him. I believe the negativity that arose this morning just happened to resemble that which I felt during our past, and like a key to a lock, opened my memory of his name. (Later, when back in Minnesota, I would reconnect with him and make amends for my mistakes.)

I heard music emanating from somewhere down below in the thicket of Yangshuo. It actually resembled marching band music, and it sounded like it was coming straight off the record player—some crackles in there for effect. Somehow, it made for an appropriate soundtrack and—for whatever reason—it brought to mind a loon's call on a quiet lake.

My life isn't complicated, yet up here with that cawlming view and the release of negative emotion, I realized just how tightly I maintain myself, keeping captive the peace hidden beneath that a place like Yangshuo had the ability to reveal. I slowly, carefully, descended the wet steps, returned to my bike, and pedaled the smaller streets through the drizzle, eventually finding my way onto the main road out of town and toward the Yulong River.

Fresh and energized from the morning meditation, my legs rotated the fixed-gear bike. Leaving behind the traffic and buildings of the city, and now riding past the rock and greens feeling positive and free, I was reminded that, like snow, rain is more appealing in the countryside.

This gang of other travelers I met were enjoying themselves as well.

The thought struck me that this was why I loved playing in the rain as a child. When you let go and accept the rain, it really is stimulating.

Soon I reached the municipality's edge:

As I was photographing the scenery near here, another example of local life emerged as an old woman waved and yelled at me from across the street. Then she approached and demonstrated her sales skills to peddle some petals.

I couldn't resist, so hopped off my pedals to look at her flowers.

Then I heard another voice from across the street and looked back up.

I'd like to think it was a hobby for these ladies to greet tourists, but chances are they needed the income. I bought some postcards and a crown of flowers traditional for these parts.

The river was near. Past these ladies, I rode on for another mile or so until coming to a parking lot-like landing where tourists gathered, awaited boat rides, and locals stood at their service. Men unloaded boats for the tours in a fashion I hadn't seen before.

I looked enviably at these motorless bamboo boats.

I wanted to be all Mark Twain and experience "Life on the Yulong". However, I was biking this day. From here, I pedaled along a small road with the river to my right. A mile or two later, I hopped off my bike at a clearing and stood on the Yulong's soft, grassy bank. In a dreamy scene, mist hovered above the smooth water of the wide river that flowed before the backdrop of a giant rock-wall. The slightest of drizzles rapped against my rain jacket as I scanned the right-to-left flow. Soon a bamboo raft approached, gracefully skimming across the surface. The driver navigated by standing in the rear and pushing a long pole against the shallow river bottom. Two passengers sat toward the front on a seat, enjoying a tour of this scenery via the smooth movement and almost pure silence of this man/river-powered locomotion. It was "cawlming."

It was also telling. I took in a few more meditative moments surveying before looking down below the bank to see small, freshwater fish darting in the clear water above a rocky bottom. I found the scene so enticing and perfect that there existed both the curiosity to touch and feel and "be" it by putting my hand in the current, all the while admiring and content not to touch a thing. I had already realized this weekend the ways nature can affect me. Right here on this bank, though, I felt how nature "is" me—perhaps that part of me linked to the days when humans existed with little choice but to embrace or defend against whatever elements they were in. Anymore, it's rare to awaken this part of my mind as I live in a setting heavily influenced by the mind's accompanying drive to invent, build, and create—a need that has modified the natural drastically.

Standing along the Yulong reignited the at-home feeling of being where humans haven't manipulated the environment. And then it occurred to me the resistance to combine the two human fulfillments of 1) being with nature and 2) manipulating it. I'd rather walk a dirt path through the woods than a concrete one; likewise, I was a little let down when a wooden bridge in a nature reserve in China turned out to be plastic "wood." Perhaps this explains why American consumers think so highly of "natural" products. Combating my previous assumptions of it being environmental health, I theorized this phenomenon to be why I didn't like seeing a piece of paper in an otherwise clean forest at that reserve. It just looked "wrong"—though it wasn't hurting anything. Perhaps this fundamental clash of keeping the technical and natural separate isn't something all people have—or have to varying degrees. Considering that many in China (and Vietnam and Cambodia) didn't seem to experience this clash, I could lighten up on why they'd litter with less concern. It simply didn't bother them as long as it wasn't unhealthy. If I didn't like it, I was the one with the problem.

Even inside one of China's most important historic sites, the Forbidden City, I'd discover that litter is not, well, forbidden.

I walked back to my bike, hopped on the wet seat, and proceeded through more earthly delight. In fact, nearing the end of the river road, I ventured through what I considered to be the best shot of this landscape.

I don't know how these giants were created. I'd guess geologists would say these are old mountains as their sediment has flaked off and collected at their base. I would have loved to have had a geologist with me at the time.

This scene was the finale of this route. Soon after, the path met another main highway straight south of town. So I started pedaling back north. When getting to the city's edge, I decided to explore more of it by venturing off the beaten path. My final impression of Yanghsuo would be a human one.

I took a right onto a street that sliced through some businesses and then bridged the Li River. I entered an area of plain, drab apartment buildings, looked to the right, and scanned this neighborhood from the elevated vantage point of the road. Then I took advantage of gravity and let it pull me down a narrow street into this neighborhood. I stopped to watch three women of varied age cooking outdoors along the street.

Now that I could say a few things in Mandarin, I introduced myself and asked what was cooking. It was zong zi (*zòng zi*, 粽子):

Rice cooked in a large leaf with bean (or other filling) in the center

And this area man couldn't wait to get him some:

I myself enjoyed the warm, soft—albeit bland—meal, said *xiè xie*, and biked back up the narrow street. Nearing the main road, I stopped to watch these boys:

The townspeople of Yangshuo offered their own distinct, small town definition of urban Han Chinese.

As much a statement about the natural, this journey to Yangshuo was bookended with a representation of the human experience in China.

After this, I returned to my hostel, cleaned up, and enjoyed a final dinner with Lucy and Reynold. The next morning we drove back to Zhuhai.

Yangshuo's features resonated a variety of emotional and educational notes, all coming together for a lovely chord.

***

The Seemingly Arbitrary Nature of Wealth

A dichotomous element of China (indeed, of all the world) was evidenced again soon after I got back to Zhuhai. Later in April, TPR needed to create a new batch of brochures and pamphlets. I was asked to be the too-happy-to-believe model that makes learning English look like winning the lottery. It was a fun time, but also a powerful one as it coincided with another experience I had within days of the shoot.

Mary, a twenty-something fellow English teacher from Kansas, joined in as the other English teacher on camera. Naturally, students came as well. The ten-year-old boy was handsome with a new haircut, and the three girls of varied age were all prettied up and ready to dazzle. Our group piled into a school van and took the twenty-minute ride to the photographer's studio/apartment in Gongbei. We entered his "studio"—the living room now held make-up bags, snacks, and water; the dining room housed a white backdrop set; the kitchen contained the lighting equipment; and the photographer readied, aimed, and fired. The modeling commenced with the children going first.

The camera clicked, lights flashed, and models moved from one "I'm cool, learning is fun" pose to the next.

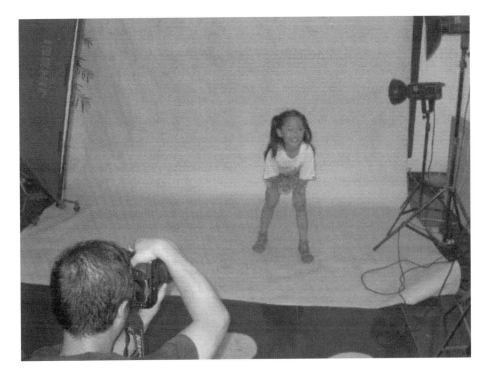

This scene was lively with a hint of glam—strikingly dissimilar to the one I witnessed just a few days prior.

In the middle of a spring day in Zhuhai, I approached the bus stop along the main road in my neighborhood. Bus stops are busy places where people carry change so were hotspots for folks seeking charity. There weren't twenty children crowding around you for cash as you might imagine in some poor countries. Here, it was the guy with no legs or an old woman—maybe one or two at each stop.

For the more expressive, another customary alms-seeking strategy was to set up a karaoke machine minus the TV and sing to the enjoyment (or not) of those walking by or waiting around. Most often it was a man or woman in need due to medical reasons for them or their children. This day, I heard the voice of a small child while approaching the bus stop.

Behind mom seemed an appropriate backdrop of rubble and debris from a building renovation. The two had written in front of them the reason for their predicament. I couldn't read it, but if it was like others I'd asked the translations of, it described the hardship they were going through.

At the modeling studio, girls were being paid to have people photograph them, while this little girl on the street was begging for some attention. The models were given food and drink to make sure they were comfortable and relaxed; this girl and her mom were seeking money, I assume, to buy food and drink. The models were in a studio; this girl was standing before a pile of demolished concrete. Yet what was the difference between these two performers? They may have had similar young talents, but for some reason one was coddled and the other begging.

The drastic and seemingly random nature of this situation had me think upon the bigger picture, and doing so created a bridge between this situation and countless others. This is about all the seemingly nonsensical leaps in prosperity: one good author's book goes viral, another's doesn't; a singer goes from lounges to stadiums practically overnight; one of many Internet startups takes off; the athlete gifted with a great golf swing is rich, whereas the athlete gifted with an ability to deadlift just gets by.

A terse and convenient statement sums this all up as "life isn't fair." But such a curt response troubled me. It implies an existence under the clutches of a world stacked against you. While some people are dealt tougher cards in the hand of life, I realized a concurrent truth: all things being equal—and given the factors we can/may control such as hard work, education, financial decisions—we don't know why some people/things become successful. The recipients of the spoils are deserving, but it's an elusive and fickle process.

We may be in a world currently and perhaps forever marred by such inconsistencies, but rather than seeing this little girl as the victim of an unfair and cruel world, I realized this apparent randomness is a natural constant to acknowledge throughout everyone's life. And on this level, the results are out of our control. Conscious of this, I suddenly felt the weight of how serious people take such matters: threatened/jealous of another's success, guilty for having more money than others, or shame when they fail. But worth isn't determined by success if, in fact, success is determined—at least partially—by something out of our hands.

***

Two Hong Kongs

Over the weekend of May 1st, I went back to Hong Kong. This visit demonstrated China's diversity via the human rainbow in Hong Kong's Kowloon district. As well, it demonstrated its economic diversity—and at a most poetic time: this weekend was the Labor Day holiday commemorating the working class.

This time, I found a place to stay in Kowloon—the dense, multi-ethnic area across the channel from Hong Kong Island.

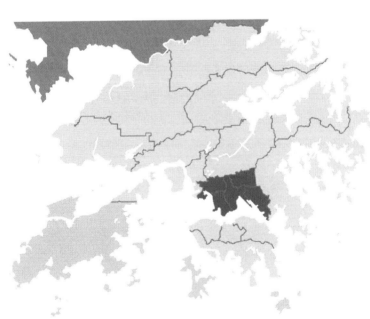

Kowloon in dark green (wikipedia.org)

Big Texan Jim, the restaurateur, recommended a hotel, giving me a name and phone number on a small piece of paper like it was on the down-low. It *felt* like I was getting a good deal, but who knows? At least it was affordable, which, for a guy making Chinese money to say about Hong Kong prices, means something.

Starting off in the late afternoon, I took the ferry from the same Zhuhai port, but this time landed on the Kowloon side of the channel. I walked a handful of blocks through a neighborhood becoming ever more crowded with people, cars, and attention-grabbing storefronts. I arrived at a large building with the deceptive name Chungking Mansions. It was a high-rise, and my hotel was just a section of a floor of this bustling building that housed several small, independent operations comprised of drab, dorm-sized rooms. Its main entrance was wide open for customers of the many main floor vendors selling phones, food, snacks, and more.

Business owners, employees, customers, and those just hanging out pretty much all seemed to be of the central Asian, Middle-Eastern, or African variety. Hong Kong is known for being West-meets-East. Here in Kowloon, though, it's World-meets-East. And Chungking Mansions was smack-dab in the middle of it all.

The view out its front entrance

The next morning, I decided to go to Central, the neighborhood I toured my first time here, as there were some things I never got to see then. Leaving the busy blocks near my hotel for the ferry to take me across the channel, things in Kowloon took an interesting twist. Along the right hand side of the street, I began to pass a figurative parade of luxury with floats of wealthy citizens. A row of designer shops made for an impressive stretch of street in Kowloon—and a convenient one for high-end shoppers this Labor Day weekend.

Gucci

No need to be embarrassed. We've all got our guilty pleasures. Yours is Prada; mine is Sears watches.

These shoppers were on display because the stores only let in so many at a time.

LV

Brandon Ferdig

When I took these pictures, I thought back to the previous fall when a student of mine—Rena, from that first adult class—was reading a book about traveling to America. Written in English from a Chinese perspective, it read (my paraphrase): "In America, they always try to sell you something. Everything is designed to get you to be a consumer." I talked to a couple college-aged guys in one of these luxury lines. Over from the mainland, they said they like to come here to shop. While that book pointed out America's consumerism, mainlanders hop to Westernized Hong Kong on the holiday honoring the working man for a taste of some of that delicious high-end commerce.

After speaking with the young guys, I approached the ferry port where I boarded the vessel taking me and other riders to Central. Despite it being a government holiday, the lack of commotion inside the skyway surprised me. There was also no traffic on the street below, but I could see people out on the sidewalks. Making my way down, I saw tan women sitting on blankets on the sidewalks—some even in the streets—talking, playing cards, and eating from picnic baskets. Perhaps back on the mainland, Chinese laborers celebrated this way, but here in wealthier and Westernized Hong Kong it was these women playing that role. But who were these women?

Hong Kong blocks the streets to give the workers their reign. And in Central, these blocks were owned by Filipinas.

Filipinos, as these people are generally known, is the English term for those who currently inhabit the archipelago nation east of China, the Philippines. They come to Hong Kong in much the same capacity as Latinos to the United States: to offer their labor for much higher wages than they can get back home. Interestingly, both Latinos and Filipinos are populations formerly colonized and heavily influenced by Spain.

After making their acquaintance, I continued this unorthodox tour of Hong Kong: this once-a-year replacement of the everyday business bustle with these festive Filipinas. Entering Statue Square, the urban plaza near the Legislative Council Building, I stopped to check out another group picnicking along a table under the shade of a canopy. This time, I was offered a place to sit and a plateful of some of their vittles.

The pasta salad was remarkably reminiscent of the kinds of paper-plate portions I'd dish up at my childhood church picnics. The rice, however, was spiced considerably different than Mom's wild rice dishes back in Minnesota.

While eating, I asked where all the men were. Some talked about how the men were out doing their own thing, but I gathered that there simply weren't many Filipino men around. (I knew a couple Filipinas in Zhuhai who, themselves, came to China alone and sent money back home.) Some of these women also had children who were back with Grandma, or perhaps Dad, while Mommy was away to help ensure her kids had a better life. Many worked here in Hong Kong as housecleaners or caretakers of others' children, adding a sad irony to the situation. It struck me as unfair—or least exemplary of the random, inconsistent aspect of the world we live in. But the way these women see it, they are grateful Hong Kong is here to provide them this better alternative. They told me it beats what's waiting for them in the Philippines.

So far from home, it was nice to see all the company and support among them.

Later this day, I went to the Hong Kong aviary and enjoyed all the interesting and up-close birds. At the end of the tour I saw a Filipina walking along with, and looking after, this Chinese boy:

Too bad she couldn't have off for Labor Day, but I offered her a reprieve by playing big brother with the young man. I reached for some berries in a nearby tree, and we tossed them at the content pelican resting below.

The Filipinas weren't the only foreign minority here working hard to try and make a better living. Around my hotel in Kowloon were many young Indian men who had arrived with entrepreneurial mindsets to sell their tailoring services, knock-off watches, or run restaurants and inexpensive hotels. They marketed themselves—aggressively. In an apparent perpetuation of competition amongst each other, I once had five young salesmen approach me one right after the other within a block-and-a-half to sell their services or goods.

"No." "Nope." "No thanks." "Sorry." "Not interested."

I got to know one such salesman—tall, thin, dressed in slacks and off-white button-up, with a smart face—while waiting outside my hotel building's entrance. He said he came from India in the not-too-distant past, had an "in" with a friend working here, and somehow stayed in Hong Kong with seemingly little concern about immigration. He was working right there on the sidewalk—had just tried to sell me a fitted suit. I don't think these guys rake it in, and it's tough work selling like they do. In response to their in-your-face sales, it might not be as easy to empathize with their journey. Nonetheless, they come here for the same reason those Filipinas do: to escape poverty and have a chance for a better life.

Waiting for his chance. I thought if these guys could tone it down a notch they'd be a hit in Minnesota where many salespeople struggle to get over that fear of rejection.

Indeed, it seemed that, made up of the Indian, Filipina, and perhaps the other Middle Eastern, West African, and other peoples around, this was a class that could encompass one of "Two Hong Kongs."

Interestingly, just as mainland China is 93 percent Han, so is Hong Kong. You wouldn't guess that in Kowloon, though.

Nonetheless, it was the Chinese who were the overwhelming ingredient in the human mélange called Hong Kong: Chinese with a Western twist.

Doing the Argentine Tango

(Or at least Chinese with a *Hong Kong* twist.) I'd never see these kinds of gestures on the mainland:

Relating to my question during my December visit on what it is that makes Hong Kong prosperous, I realized this time that knowing a city is knowing its people.

***

Chapter Twelve: Gambling and Sex

Odds Are, You'll Love Macau's Casinos

Gambling was not a significant activity for me. I played once and won the equivalent of about $25. However, mentioning Macau without bringing up their casinos is like talking about Hollywood without mentioning movies. Even if you're not a gambling fan, the rise of this industry in Macau is noteworthy—scratch that—it is amazing.

Macau is the biggest gambling spot in the world. It quintuples the gaming revenue of Las Vegas. While China has developed in recent years, and though I did often see cash card games on the sidewalks of Zhuhai, Macau remains the only spot in China where gambling is legal—courtesy of Portuguese policy starting in the mid-1800s. Thus, all this massive nation's casinos are packed into this speck on the map:

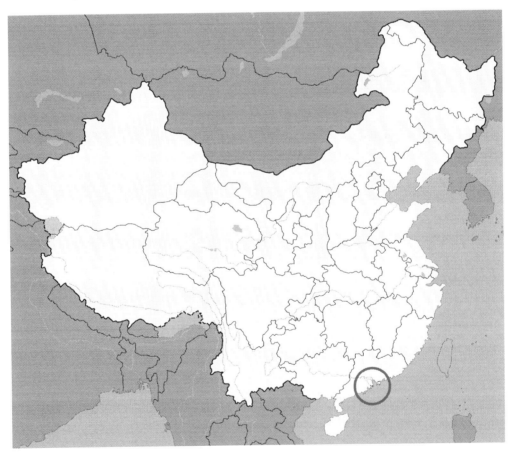

Soon after Hong Kong, I revisited my other Western respite. On this April weekday mid-morning, I wasn't too early this time to catch a casino bus from Bordergate to Coloane Island. On the bridge, we passed by some of the casinos on the peninsula.

Not the best day out. Guess it was a good one to do something indoors.

Macau's thirty-three casinos are sprinkled along the southeast coast of the Macau peninsula and along the Cotai strip—reclaimed land that used to be the strait between Taipa and Coloane islands. They are patronized almost entirely by Chinese traveling from Hong Kong and all over the mainland. Their favorite game is baccarat, a Blackjack style of card game but with different scoring and drawing rules.

Over the bridge, we stopped on the Cotai Strip where three examples of Macau's new mega-casinos stood among others.

City of Dreams

The Galaxy

Then, a name familiar to most Americans came into view: The Venetian.

Outside it, a moat surrounded the city-like exterior.

Inside was more of the "city," but first was just your everyday, ho-hum lobby.

Now let's go to town.

Outside or inside?

Outside or inside? Statue or person?

Along with the gaming and shopping came the concerts, theater, and sporting events. The City of Dreams offered an inexpensive and unique theater experience that takes IMAX to a new level. Onlookers stand on the floor underneath a dome that itself is an enormous semi-spherical screen featuring some stunning graphic and colorful dragons swimming with whales or flying through the air.

Walking into the main entrance of the Wynn Casino, I was greeted with a forty-foot-wide, cordoned-off mound interrupting the lobby floor. As the top of this midday hour approached, people started gathering around ready with cameras. Soon the lights of the large lobby flickered and dimmed. Then red light shone onto the mound and smoke rose from between its cracks as it began to split apart and a Chinese melody began echoing out.

The slices receded into the floor, revealing a giant hole filled with smoke and a large shape below.

The giant began to rise. An enormous dragon dauntingly ascended, pivoting upon its platform.

I was then struck by the most interesting sight or sound of the whole presentation: "taps" coming from the dragon. One from the left, a couple from the right, scattered but consistent. Then I caught someone causing the noise by tossing a coin. Though I didn't take part in the monetary acknowledgment, I understood where these folks were coming from. But as quickly as it rose to power, it descended back into its lair. After only a few minutes, the music stopped, the lights returned to normal, and the dome closed, leaving some residual smoke floating out of its cracks like a recently put-out campfire. I guess it was time to get back to the slots.

What makes all this more amazing is that until 2002, a government-induced monopoly prevented foreign-owned casinos. So all these complexes exist courtesy of American, Australian, and Hong Kong (and Macanese) developers and have been built in just the last ten years.

Now onto some sex. I had heard that prostitutes were abundant in Macau. One friend back in Minnesota told me about a presence of Russian ladies if you're into that. It wasn't on my docket. That afternoon I was meeting with Australian Paul and our mutual friend, American George, the attorney who introduced Paul and I back in the fall. We planned to get coffee, but they asked me if I'd ever seen "the parade." I hadn't. I hadn't any idea what they were talking about; they were eager to show me.

We walked into an older, pre-2002 casino that looked like a place the Rat Pack would've partied in. I remember red velvet and mirrors in the lobby. The hallways were narrower and cozier than the spacious corridors of the new wave of casinos. We took the stairway on the left side of the entry and headed down to a hallway that curved around a dining area. Separated by the curved wall with large windows, diners sat inside having coffee, and we joined in at our own table. Looking out through the windows to the hallway, I noticed a vendor selling magazines and snacks. The combination of the eatery and the little convenience shop actually reminded me of a college campus student union.

Moments later I was looking down attending to my tea. Meanwhile, Paul kept his attention on the hallway. I looked back up and saw a couple pretty, young women walking by. They wore cleavage-revealing tops, miniskirts, and had their faces and hair all done up. I thought Paul was just being Paul staring at a couple cute women. But look-alikes kept coming. I put two and two together and assumed this to be the "parade" they spoke of, yet maintained disbelief as I asked, "Are they prostitutes?" My friends nodded. It was two in the afternoon. I had my tea, children dined with their parents, the vendor guy sold a pack of chewing gum—and hookers walked by. Though they looked incredibly out of place, I was apparently the only one to think so.

It was, in fact, about fifteen women who walked to one end of the hallway, turned around, walked back along and around the curved wall, and then came back again. They never stopped moving, and I'd later learn from a Portuguese Macanese reporter that this is because it helps them skirt the law. Prostitution is defined in Macau as soliciting in a stationary location. By moving around, even just pacing back and forth, they could apparently claim to be just "walking by."

Paul and George speculated that these women probably come from the mainland and tell their families they're working as waitresses. Paul, who had actually paid for one of these women before, added that the Macanese mafia ran this casino and sex racket. Most of the johns are Chinese. Whites get charged double, Paul said.

[Prostitution went both ways. One night at one of the two Western bars in Zhuhai, I pulled a stool up next to some Irish regulars. One clean-shaven middle-aged man with shoulder-length curly blonde locks was having a beer with friends. I got to know him a little, and he offered his profession: a pimp. But he wasn't rounding up Chinese women for hire. Chinese women were his clients; Western men were his product. He didn't seem rough enough to fit the stereotype of pimps back home, but with a cigarette in his mouth, a large frame, and a pleasant face, he looked right for this role in China, hustling up his troops to make sure the Chinese women were satisfied—and paid up.]

After leaving the company of Paul and George, I wandered the casinos a bit more before ending this excursion the same way it started: hopping on the casino shuttle taking me right back to the border.

Thousands come to Macau each day to tickle that reward center in the brain. This urge is so strong it funds these palaces and attracts the highest-end retailers to set up shop within their opulent corridors. It stimulates the entertainment, sex, and, I'm guessing, recreational drug industry in Macau. Casinos really are houses of hedonism and forts of fantasy. Then again, they're also just a place for old ladies to come play coin slots. I guess, like anything, this thrill is one that can go to extraordinary, exaggerated levels—or simply be used to have some fun.

With all the interest in gaming in China and the resultant boom in prosperity brought to Macau, I wondered if other Chinese cities wished to get in on some of this risky revenue. I simultaneously wondered if other cities are relieved to not have to worry about gambling and the potential problems that come with it.

***

Sex Ed

According to some of my male colleagues, my final adult class that started in April was the best time and place to teach at TPR. It was the weekday, daytime shift at the Gongbei branch. These guys spoke about these classes very expressively, because whereas they typically concerned themselves with reaching the students' minds, these Gongbei afternoon classes had them focused on the student body.

I arrived my first day at that Gongbei hotel branch. Off the elevator to the fourth floor, through the glass door of our suite, past the reception desk, and down the hall, I entered my classroom. Moments later, so did they. One by one: pretty young woman after pretty young woman. As much as those male teachers were being dogs, they were right about these students being attractive. There were nine in all, the oldest in her mid-thirties—a Japanese mother, actually, whose husband was there on business.

The one second from the right was actually from Argentina. Thus, we had four major languages represented in that class.

I was self-conscious as I stood with that row of faces staring back at me. "Good afternoon. My name is Brandon. I am from the United States." I wore a half-smile with eighteen attractive eyes on me the whole time. What can I say? There was some sexual energy running through me. But having taught this curriculum before, I was able to rely on this experience and, after introductions, got down to teaching.

We continued on week in and week out. I got used to the fact that almost all these students were physically sexy. I had to. It was work, and it was my responsibility to be in work mindset. Guys may express how teaching an attractive class or having attractive female coworkers is great. But I think if more were honest, they'd admit that it isn't ideal having physical thoughts and reactions interfering with lessons or work. One red-faced instance occurred when one of the girls asked in the middle of class if I was single. It had nothing to do with the lesson. I said I was, and she responded with a resigned, "Hmm. Such a waste."

Concluding my time with them—my final class of my year—we went out as I had with my other adult classes. But instead of a restaurant and karaoke, we went to a dance bar on a Saturday night. This was more their style.

Chapter Thirteen: Apples to Apples to Oranges

The experiences comprising my final two months in Zhuhai seemed to all center around institutions: education, law enforcement, a factory, and—bridging nicely from the previous chapter—the social institution of sex.

In Your Face

Though the prostitutes in Macau were the most extreme, I encountered several examples of what I considered a high level of openness toward sexual matter.

I saw these books right out in the open at a souvenir shop.

In tourist-friendly, Yangshou, along busy, pedestrian-only West Street, a shop with all kinds of sexual devices and knickknacks was wide open for all the public.

That dress is made entirely of condoms.

Then there was the female clothing store located in the same town square as my school that I taught at on weekends. Around the store window were these eight-by-ten-inch photos:

I watched children walk by with mom and dad, paying no attention to the sex in the window.

At the Sex Shop

Then in late May, I was on a bus in Zhuhai making the same trip I had made probably a hundred times by then. I sat toward the back on the passenger's side looking out the window as we slowed for the bus stop. Suddenly I took notice of the building (or rather, the contents therein) across the sidewalk. I wondered if I wasn't just "seeing things," but darned if through those wide-open glass doors I didn't see an enormous glass phallus on the shelf. I couldn't make out anything specific. I saw there were other items on the back wall and some island displays on the shiny, off-white tiled floor. It resembled a jewelry store. The storefront was pink, and like most in this neighborhood, squeezed amidst several adjacent businesses: a bakery, a Circle K convenience store, and an electronics retailer.

Within a day or two I confirmed its identity. (This was easy because it also happened to be directly across the street from TPR headquarters.) A school worker told me it was a place people go to for sexual needs. Once again, I thought it so strange, especially because there was a school close by that had its many yellow-uniformed youth come wait here for their ride. They'd stand directly in front of those doors that revealed what did turn out to be two giant glass penises on display along the back wall. A mirror behind them reflected their appeal, might, disgust, or what have you. I was curious, so I asked Tiffany to come along to translate and see what this place was all about. This time, she was totally fine with it—noticeably less hesitant than when going to speak to the alms-seeking lady in the fall.

On one hand, the shop got more lewd than the manly monoliths, offering various dolls for men and many devices for a woman's pleasure. On the other hand, its main purpose was actually a less sexy advisory one: helping couples with their family planning. A short staircase led to a room which rested above one of the neighboring businesses. I assumed it to be where the advising took place. Out of that room came a small, skinny Chinese woman in her mid-thirties. She introduced herself to Tiffany and me as the director.

She said this city-backed institution offered a place for residents to find answers and solutions to their sexual needs and concerns. Condoms were handed out for free and other contraceptives were available for sale. As she explained her operation, a thirtyish man came in off the sidewalk as casually as if it were the bakery next door, picked up a few boxes of complimentary condoms as nonchalantly as if they were donuts, signed for them, and walked out. Nothing to it. Condoms were also available in stores as impulse purchases right next to the gum and candy.

This variety sounds terribly uncomfortable.

Toward the end of our talk, I saw some of those school kids walk right past those large, open, double doors. I asked the director if kids entering the store was a problem. It wasn't. No boys pushing their friends inside for giggles. Sometimes teenagers would come in, she said, which was fine as there were no strict rules on age, but added that the store wouldn't sell products to teens.

Not being tucked away in the shadows of an alley or behind a door with a guy checking IDs, the blow-up dolls and vibrators suddenly weren't a big deal. Context makes such a difference. *But what allowed all this sexual exposure in China to begin with?* I think that sex wasn't shied away from because it wasn't so charged—such as it is in the United States. In comparing Zhuhai to America apples to apples, it seemed that if a "10" is for those very eager to express sexuality, and a "0" designates those who are adamant about never talking about or seeing it, then America is populated with people from one end of the spectrum to the other, whereas Zhuhai had a social vibe humming somewhere in the middle.

However, I took comparing the United States to China better described as apples to oranges, because whether prude or crude, the US attitude toward sex was louder. Think Janet Jackson's wardrobe malfunction. People here, meanwhile, seemed to exist on a whole other continuum where sex just wasn't a huge issue—no matter where you were on the continuum.

Both as an indicator of China's mild manner and America's tenseness, I couldn't help but notice the apathy when a seventeen-year-old walked into a sex shop or a bar. I did wonder, though, if while no one in China giggled at the nudity, perhaps they didn't admire it as much, either; that while it was easier to talk about sex, perhaps they didn't find as much meaning in it.

[Perhaps this is an unrelated point—one not regarding reactivity, but actualization—but I also came to believe that the West's more exaggerated traits were why people here looked up to Westerners. The Chinese just didn't have someone as goofy as Jim Carrey or as athletic as Lebron James or as sexy and sultry as Kate Upton. Thus, I constantly saw locals enjoying the music, movies, and other forms of entertainment from the West. That being said, the degree to which prosperity, and its allowance for actualization, has to do with this will correspond to how much Americans' eyes may one day look toward China's celebrities as role models taking expression to new heights.]

Following the use of labels like "mild manner," these next two experiences challenged such assumptions specifically and spoke to the nature of stereotypes in general.

***

The Other Side of Servile

Sometime in May, my retired Australian expat friend, Paul, sat down with me at a coffee shop inhaling his cigarette and exhaling smoke with concern in his eyes and his breathing. Right away—perhaps after offering his usual, "How's it goin', mate?"—he shared that his wife, the one who treated him like a king and who by now was the mother to his daughter, had threatened to take their newborn and never see him again if he didn't put his wife's name on the title of his condominium. This docile woman had changed her tune—and it set off Paul's alarm. His face expressed fear. He didn't know what to do. He was afraid of losing his only child, and he wanted the property to be willed to her. He worried that when he dies, a property in his wife's name would be in jeopardy by her eager siblings interested in moving in and taking over.

But that was the unwritten deal, I guess. Paul could have his face shaved and toenails clipped, but the price would be a significant chunk of his worth and a potential conflict with his wife—and her family posthumously. It seemed the financially-minded feminine MO—the one inducing these women to make the moves on Steve and Paul and then treating these men like kings—was the same motivation that pitted these women against their partners if push came to shove. The Newtonian law of equal and opposite reaction seemed to hold, and it exemplified a phenomenon I saw in a few capacities in China: opposing activity accompanying stereotyped activity.

Soon after this coffee, and similar to this submissive/dominant dichotomy on display here, was an exhibition of the compliance/rebellion continuum. My stereotype that the Chinese were largely the former made news of a protest all the more shocking.

***

Pictures from a Protest

"Hey man. There's a protest going on up the street" said my colleague, Warren, in his New Zealand accent. He approached me while I was speaking with the receptionists at our school's headquarters. I turned around to meet him.

"Really?" I responded. "Where?"

"Around the corner at that government building," Warren explained. "I was just out taking a walk, and there were all these people holding a banner and blocking the drive."

This was big news because the idea of uprisings in China brought as much curiosity to me then as it probably does to you as you read this—only I was one block away.

"What are the police doing?" I asked.

"They're just standing there next to the crowd."

If ever there was a time to explore the topic of protest in this land of censorship and alleged state brutality, it was now. Not knowing what to expect or how they'd react to me being there—taking pictures, no less—I coolly walked up to the scene. A group of demonstrators stood by...

For months I had heard from locals and expats that public gatherings were a no-no. I even heard that private get-togethers, where even just a dozen folks gathered in someone's home, were prohibited without permission. So I approached the scene with more than a hint of anxiety. Taking into account rumors I'd heard in America—via the game of "telephone" 8,000 miles long—of police brutality, cold and dark prisons, and summary executions, I expected a tense, electrified scene. Warren had said, however, that it was pretty low-key. Indeed, when I arrived, things were as described.

I encountered a peaceable crowd of approximately 150 people assembled on the sidewalk; I walked through with a don't-mind-me-just-passing-through kind of nervous, faux innocence. I half-anticipated being escorted away. So I kept an eye in my periphery for any approaching authorities—particularly as I slowed to observe...and photograph.

Protesters gathered around the entrance to a gated government building

There were no megaphones, no chants of "Hell no, we won't go!" The protesters just sat (or stood) there. They did block the entrance. Maybe that was their play. If so, I guess they let their actions do the talking—as well as this banner:

"If there are no people dying, the government doesn't care." For "living problems" the government isn't generous; they do their best to "kick out" the issues.

278

Normally at this gate, two guards stood at attention; today there were a few more calmly keeping watch. By now, this shouldn't have surprise me. Looking back at law enforcement over the year, I found them to be relaxed and approachable. During the Mid-Autumn Festival in late September part of the tradition is to release little hot-air balloons all along the coast. These are two-feet-tall, thin-paper balloons with an oil/wax canister wired beneath the open-balloon bottom. Light the oil, hold the balloon up, and watch it begin to lift itself to heights you'll be impressed by. This is done at night, and my balloon along with everyone else's along the Zhuhai coast made the stars pale by comparison.

The problem is, it was illegal here—similar to fireworks in Minnesota. And as I was lighting my second, a policeman pulled up on his scooter right next to me. "Oh man, not good," I thought and felt. Without stepping off his ride, he pointed at a piece of paper with a picture of a balloon with big red circle and line through it. I indicated him to take it, hoping that confiscation would be the worst of it. But he didn't want my paraphernalia. He waved his hand at me letting me know to keep it—just don't light it. I was surprised and relieved. He then gave an agreeable look and drove off. I thought, "Well, okay. You have a good night, too, Mr. Nice Policeman."

On another occasion in the winter, I walked past armed guards around some ATMs—the first time I saw a gun in China. I wanted a picture but half-expected a tough grimace and head-cock saying, "Get you and your camera out of here." But he just smiled goofily and posed.

Then, one month prior to the protest, my friend Jerry and I walked by this very same gated government complex that the protesters now occupied. One young, expressionless, at-attention guard stood firm in a light green military uniform and hat. I stopped and wondered if he would be like the British guards who never break face. I said hello. He smiled, said hello back, and talked to my friend Jerry and me about his job.

Maybe it's because the populace isn't armed; maybe a more homogenous population means less ethnic group tension. Maybe it's a cultural thing or less reactive personalities that make law enforcement in these parts less edgy than some in America. Whatever the reason, my initial ideas of social organization inspired by my first morning here echoed throughout the year and up to this protest: that the top of government houses the population in a social bubble, but within this bubble things are more relaxed. It seemed to create this kind of all-or-nothing policing strategy: do anything you want, just don't threaten to pop the bubble. And apparently it takes more to do so than lighting a mini-hot-air balloon or even staging a protest, to my surprise. One bubble-burster, though, was media—the oxygen to a controversy's flame. I assume this was why a foreigner with a camera turned a head or two.

After being at the protest for about a minute, I casually raised my camera as if photographing any normal sight. I figured I could get away with a couple shots before they asked me to leave. That's pretty much what happened. Right away, people did take notice.

Man in the middle is pointing me out.

I then saw officers whisper to each other and point in my direction. *That's a little unsettling.* Then some protesters behind a cordoned-off area looked my way and approached. I was caught in the middle of brief confusion when some of these men lifted the ropes for me to enter.

I wasn't sure if they wanted me to take their picture or join their cause, but I didn't bite. And as I was declining, officers approached me. With them were a couple plain-clothed men who were actually more aggressive with me than those in uniform. One asked sternly who I worked for.

"I'm a teacher," I said.

One of the plain-clothed men began escorting me away. While doing so, protesters began a human chain that crossed the street in what looked like an attempt to block traffic. My plain-clothed companion started pushing me as I tried to get a shot of that action. Looking to my left, I saw I wasn't the only one trying to capture the moment:

From inside the complex.

I was a hair nervous about this sight. I envisioned police later that day knocking on (down) my door. It never happened. I did zoom in later and was struck by just how young these guards were.

My escort was "nice" enough to follow me a good hundred feet past the brewing chaos. When I last looked back, buses were honking and cops were in the street redirecting traffic. The protesters seemed to manage a little disorder.

In a country that relies so heavily on government for morale, security, and identity, I thought there would be more reason for protest and controversy. Yet very few surfaced—or if they did, I didn't hear about them. Later that evening, I rode past the scene on my bus en route to teach. Everything was back to normal. I then called a Chinese friend to ask her to read the local news online to see if the rare protest made headlines. She found nothing. To the vast majority of the people in Zhuhai, this event did not take place. And that's pretty much how they want it here, I'm thinking.

However, the impression I got was that this wasn't purely top-down. It would have surprised me if, when sharing this experience with Chinese acquaintances, they would have acted with strong curiosity and an intent to learn more about the protesters' motives. In the fall, when first sharing with new Chinese friends about my blog, they were eager to read it—especially if the story featured them. But enthusiasm dwindled when I told them my site was blocked. I wanted to respond, "So go around the block. It's not hard." Practically all of my non-Chinese acquaintances—whether from Ireland, England, Australia, Canada, America, New Zealand, or the Philippines—had no issue getting around what's known as "The Great Chinese Firewall" which blocks common websites like Facebook, Twitter, YouTube, and various blogs. Yet all year

I met just one outspoken woman, Lucy, who was quite critical of the CCP and their grip on media. So while the Chinese showed rebellion at the protest, compliance and unity seemed to dominate.

[I realized the phenomenon of an individual (Paul's wife) or society (China) representing activity that is one slice or one plane of the sphere of human traits. Not all people fall into the stereotype, of course—such as Lucy. And for those who do, which tilts the slice in a way that leads observers to generalize accordingly (i.e. the Chinese are compliant, Chinese women are submissive), this then causes the other side of the plane to tilt in inverse manner. Thus, China's overall higher level of compliance is countered by rare and extreme acts of rebellion.

Tiananmen Square, Beijing 1989

And with his wife threatening to leave him pending her ultimatum, the generalization Paul made of her being servile didn't comfort him so much anymore. Regardless of this idea's merit, as I got to know the people here, the stereotypes broke down in lieu of a deeper understanding. The categorizations not only miss the exceptions, but they also missed the less-commonly seen tilt.]

This made comparisons of the United Stated and China interesting. One could compare apples to apples and look at the respective law enforcement approaches, independence of the citizenry, or roles in romantic relationships. They might do so and walk away thinking good or ill of China's methods and results. Their law enforcement is nicer—*better*. Citizens are more compliant with government censorship—*worse*. I'd find, however, that it was just as agreeable to view China/America comparisons as apples to oranges, that such methods and institutions and their results weren't simply better or worse, but different. And the results were two countries with different institutions that each had their own strengths and weaknesses.

***

Comparing Education Systems

In May, I taught my third "English Corner." These were community-wide, no-cost, discussion-based sessions held by my school once a month on a Saturday evening for an hour and a half. They were a nice way for my school to reach out to the community and a nice way for area folks to come test their English. More an open discussion than a lesson and lecture, we teachers were charged with leading the group in a light, talk-provoking topic. This night I chose the topic of summer activities. It seemed fitting. And from this group, I anticipated a useful range of perspectives from which to discuss swimming, biking, relaxing, and traveling one's summer away. My error, however, was that I came into the night assuming the topic to be a surefire hit with the younger ones since they have all that time off from school.

Soon after I arrived this Saturday evening at the Jida branch, class started to assemble. The group consisted of seven individuals of varied age. On the upper end were a middle-aged man working in management and a couple other similarly-aged career women. There was a twenty-something blue-collar gentleman, and then the others were a school-aged mix of young women ages sixteen, fifteen, and twelve—the twelve-year-old being the daughter of one of the career women.

Soon after introducing the topic, the fifteen- and sixteen-year-olds—both impressively smart and mature—shared that they don't have an extensive summer break. They said the older students are, the less time off they have in the summer. So for them, it wasn't three months but three weeks. (The twelve-year-old had about two months off.) The sixteen-year-old could even recall the dates saying, "Last year it was July fourteenth to August fifth."

I had known in the back of my head that Chinese students went to school longer, but even despite having been here for several months at this point, that fact didn't sink in until I heard it straight from the source. And even then I had to ask a qualifier: Were the school days in June and July halftime or less? Nope—although the school subjects change during the summer, they said. So just when I thought they'd be anticipating the end of the school year, these two were right in the middle of their longest span between breaks: January—February for Chinese New Year and July—August for summer.

To Chinese upperclassmen, school feels more like a career, and when I did the math, I found they attend class about eighty more days a year than Minnesota students. Upon calculating this, I thought about the alarm back in America regarding how Chinese students are outperforming their American counterparts and are a threat to American students' chances of finding work in this global job market. The year I was in China, in fact, students from Shanghai competed in a world-wide competency test and took the top scores across the board. I actually brought this up in class. But the fifteen-year-old retorted that though there are many smart graduates, there aren't many leaders coming out of the Chinese schools. Seen in this light, I realized the parallel truth that comparing the two systems is, again, also like comparing apples and oranges.

In the days surrounding this English Corner, I had happened to be working on an article on ways for American kids to stay sharp during the summer break so they can hit the ground running come the next fall. While thinking about what kids can do over this time, I realized the *opportunity* this time away from school can be for young people. In my youth, I worked at my father's automotive repair shop and earned a little money. For today's eager, adventurous, and industrious youth, work can be tricky as labor laws prevent kids from getting jobs, but technology has compensated by opening doors to work, knowledge, and projects in limitless amounts online. Plus, there are volunteering and community and outdoor activities available. Young people can exercise their interests and initiative in countless ways that promote their growth, accomplishment, and identity, and increases a sense of self-respect and responsibility. Of course, summer is also the chance for kids to get lazy, get bored, get into trouble, and forget all they learned. But America has benefited—and been defined—by outside-the-system endeavors of motivated individuals. China, it seems, has risen dramatically over the last twenty years as a people who stress procedure, labor, and unity over expression, curiosity, and leadership.

[Whether you see the two systems as apples to apples or apples to oranges might determine your response to seeing city buses full of Chinese high-schoolers heading to their schools on a Sunday night to start the week. The apples to apples person might say, "Boy, are they preparing for success." The other person, seeing the students all dressed identically in blue-and-white uniforms, might respond, "Boy, are these young adults being institutionalized." But perhaps more important than which side you lean is the consideration: "Why does it have to be one way or the other?" We like to have our ideological preference be the norm for all, but if someone prefers more regiment or a more relaxed approach, we can create educational institutions that function under varying amounts of either.]

After the discussion, we went back to talking about summer activities.

***

One China

The "One China" mantra describes more than their universalized school system. It can explain China's historic and present creations of the most impressive large work projects: The Great Wall, Terra Cotta Warriors, Three Gorges Dam, the Hong Kong to Macau bridge, and the Beijing Olympics 2008 Opening Ceremony. This mindset also appeared to come into play on the job.

Sometimes I'd enter my gym, walk into the workout area, and see through the glass wall of the yoga room a supervisor standing before two rows of at-attention employees. He'd pace a little while speaking, stop to address his workers, and then wait for the response they'd declare back to him. Witnessing this early in my year, I just thought this gym was a particularly tight ship. But I'd see this pattern replicated.

At the grocer

At the golf course

At a hotel

But remember, this is China. Like the security guard and the soldier, they also know how to keep it light.

Then in the spring, I met an English teacher named Twigy who taught at a factory. I asked to see this example of One China at work, and she agreed to show me.

***

Chinese Factory & Workers

In June I went to see how China's unity played out at a factory. Conversely, it taught me to appreciate the individuals behind the scenes who make the world's products. Though it was just one of countless factories in China, it at least offered some idea to recall next time I heard about the ominous "factory in China." Sweat shops? No breaks? Boss with a whip looking over eight-year-olds' shoulders? At least not where I went.

The factory was forty-five minutes west of Zhuhai's city center. Out here, you could tell the highway was built before the development—rather than vice-versa back in the city. There, things were cozy with the corridors knifing through neighborhoods. Out here, the large highways waited for some body around their skeletal network. There was a sense of emptiness. It reminded me of the desolation of the American West: hilly, dry land under bright sun. But rather than Old West towns, this frontier was citified with industrial parks. Big manufacturers took advantage of Zhuhai's SEZ status.

The bus hung a right down a smaller road and approached the campus of Flextronics. First were the signs of factory campus life—restaurants, convenience shops, little cell phone stores. These were the outskirts of the Chinese twenty-first-century boom town, seeded not in mining or railroad, but manufacturing. Hanging a quick left, the small businesses gave way to the campus proper. "Campus" is a term most commonly associated with college, so this would actually be fairly appropriate here. Cracked basketball courts sprawled to the right of the bus. Beyond them were the dormitories.

I got off the bus right here and walked ahead to the security gate. Above it, "Flextronics" was written in big, white letters on the blue canopy.

Flextronics isn't a household name—probably because they're a company for companies, making components for products from big name electronics-makers like Sony, Microsoft, and Motorola.

Beyond the gate were the offices and factories, but first I had to pass security. This tough guy greeted me at the entrance:

Intellectual property concerns require a pretty tight ship.

A couple more guards were in the security booth, and a couple others were across the road on the exit side. I entered this booth, signed my name, and awaited my guide. There was an issue with me having my laptop, but it was resolved without any problems. Then Twigy approached to take me away.

Office buildings and factories straddled each side of the road we walked along. If the pristine lawns, comfortable offices, and state-of-the-art amenities define the best work campuses in Silicon Valley, then dry grounds, plain offices, and metal-tray cafeterias of Flextronics would indicate that first/third world split once more. But I was impressed considering what the implications of a "factory in China" were supposed to be.

Building more housing: in all, Flextronics in Zhuhai houses some 5,000 workers.

A common thread between this campus and the American version was the community feel. But while a dedicated worker at Google might sleep one night at his desk, here most of the workers rarely leave at all. It's the migrant-worker culture. Few having cars and a willingness to come from long distances meant staying here basically 24/7 is the thing to do. It's insular, but it's convenient, and most of the employees are young and single. So all you students reading this who wish you'd never have to graduate and leave the campus life–here you go. And with all the small businesses nearby, it makes for a comfy little campus town.

My visit coincided with lunch, the perfect opportunity to talk to an employee.

Office staff on lunch

I approached a front-line worker: a fairly short, young man with thin, puffy hair and a polite smile. With the help of Twigy, he shared that he hailed from the province adjacent to the north of Guangdong—Hunan. He started working at Flextronics a year and a half earlier, introduced by a friend who also worked here. He was single, but said many of his male coworkers were not and so send money back home to their wives and kids. Others arrive as a family and are provided housing for this situation. And a few, naturally, meet their spouses here.

He said he missed his family, so he enjoyed going home twice a year. I'm not sure about his goals in life, but for now he seemed content to rest his lot here.

*[Some assume the exploitation of these employees. It occurred to me that the willingness for these workers to travel so far indicates the degree to which they **could** be exploited: both because they face worse alternatives back home and because of how far away they are from home. Plus, people get attached to their jobs. So while it's convenient to argue such clean-cut reasoning as, "A worker in China can quit if abused or not paid well," or "They never had to take the job in the first place," this line of thinking doesn't appreciate the gravity of a job—the way we orbit around the places of our employment in thought, emotion, and action. And it certainly doesn't take into account the exaggeration of these factors in China and places like it because the alternatives for these workers may be little more than subsistence agriculture. The option for some young parents and young singles looking to improve their (or their children's) standard of living through this kind of work, though technically a choice, is practically compulsory.*

The potential for exploitation, though—the reasons workers want these jobs so badly—also reveals the benefit of these factories. That the workers are willing to go so far for the pay they get, indicates the large improvement to their lifestyle that factory jobs/nanny jobs/sales jobs, etc., provide. Realizing this, it seems odd to speak poorly of the factories or to consider the employees victims. The stereotype that factory workers in China are abused—though I assume not false—is born out of an image of a factory I would not see here, and I believe is born out of the idea of spending a day in the factory worker's shoes without considering their hearts and minds. To speak poorly of these workers' situations is often to take aim at life's best option for them.]

After our brief chat, I followed the workers to the cafeteria and joined in for lunch.

Afterwards, Twigy and I went to visit the factory floor. We entered the manufacturing complex, where a female security guard wearing her red beret waited just inside the entrance.

Twigy got the okay, but they reminded me that no photography was allowed.

We pivoted to the right and caught these employees now off for lunch:

We entered where they came from.

This ordinary-sized entry way gave way to the extraordinary-sized floor. Rows of big, neutrally-colored, noisy machines rested upon the smooth, concrete floor and below a thirty-foot ceiling. Large banners hung overhead and across the corridors, reading generic bi-lingual sayings, such as "The Customer is Always Right."

Employees walked among the machines that were pumping and grinding out black plastic parts the workers were tasked to inspect. I focused on one large compactor-type machine that had an independent, rotating component the size of an easy chair. Its two ends would clap together vertically then pivot and separate, spitting out a freshly molded football-sized hunk of black plastic. I touched one in a nearby box; it was warm.

Workers took razor blades to the new product to shave off edges and make sure they were tip-top. The pieces were to be installed in printers. These large machines, themselves, were made by Hewlett Packard. (Makes me wonder what machines make the machines, and then, how all this industrialization got started. How did humans go from dirt, plants, and rocks, to skyscrapers, bullet trains, and emails?)

We exited this floor, headed down a wide hallway, and hung a right into a cooled room full of large, dense metal cubic hunks. They reminded me of cylinder heads on an automobile engine, where a good amount of the piece is just solid metal—only these pieces before us were the size of end tables. They were the molds that shaped the plastic parts, the shape of the mold etched into a level plane on the piece. Perfect, sharp 90s highlighted their precision. I bet I would have cut my finger running it along the edges. Some molds had metal tags bolted on that were stamped "Microsoft."

[In a country known for uncooperative intellectual property standards it surprised me that so many companies trust factories in China with their secrets. I'd heard these companies do a lot of the info-sensitive manpower stateside before sending the products over to China for assembly. Yet somewhere something seemed to get out because iPhone knock-offs were plentiful and inexpensive (and lousy). But apparently, all this copying is outweighed by the draw of good labor, a good price, and business-friendly policy—and who would've thought this in Communist China?]

Made in China, sold in China

The last room we entered was an enormous space that contained four elephant-sized machines. Large spools behind the machines unrolled shiny sheet metal about eighteen inches wide into their back ends. Halfway through the machine, a giant punch visibly stamped and stomped and shaped the heck out of the sheet metal. The "puncher" itself was about four feet wide and within it were six different stamps. With each punch, the sheet shuffled forward to the next stamp, accomplishing progressive effects to the metal—from a few indentations at the beginning to an independently cut and shaped product at the end.

At the exit, coming out the front, workers collected the items for inspection. They were familiar-looking pieces that would contribute to something resembling this:

Out came one of these specific, flat pieces with holes and grooves for various modification for the internal components of a computer tower.

After this room, the tour and day at Flextronics came to an end. I said goodbye to Twigy and waited at the bus stop outside the security gate. Thankfully, she'd have me back.

Teaching English at the Factory

One cool perk of working at Flextronics was educational opportunities. And on two occasions following my first visit, Twigy invited me out here to help lead her company's "English Club."

I arrived on an evening shortly after my visit with a couple other teachers in tow—Brian, a fortyish, thin, white Canadian guy with glasses, goatee, and an accent that was spot on; and William, an older British bloke with smooth white hair, a gentle smile, and an accent that was spot on. Twigy showed us into a large room on the third floor of one of the office buildings on campus. In this double-sized classroom, fifty students or more sat at six large, round tables. It was once more a collegiate atmosphere at this workplace, only here the students were ages 25-30 instead of 18-22. And instead of it being just another class, these after-hours employees treated this more like a social.

A couple weeks before, I was able to tour a college as well. I checked out the athletic facilities.

I went into the library.

I had lunch where I said hello to these guys:

Then, I finished the tour by sitting in on a Contract Law lecture.

To my surprise, friends of mine who taught at nearby colleges reported a fair amount of lethargy and lack of motivation from college students.

There was no lack of enthusiasm back at Flextronics.

We teachers each took a table where eager-to-participate student-workers sat around and led a discussion about the week's given topic. One time it was favorite books, another time about films. Here was my group on book night:

There's Brian the Canadian back there with his group.

Most students' choice book gravitated to one of a few classic Chinese dramas. One of these was also the subject for the second activity of the night: putting on a skit. My group retold the story of a popular Chinese love story involving an attorney who had to defend the lover of the woman the attorney loved. Like all good, classic love sagas this one ends tragically.

As usual, I learned a lot while teaching. First and foremost, these individuals countered the image imbedded in my mind when hearing the phrase "Chinese factory worker."

[I learned it's so easy to hold false ideas. In Minneapolis I've gotten more than a few misunderstood, pitying looks from strangers when sharing the size of Blackduck, my hometown. "How did you get by?" the look says as they ponder a population of 700 and then follow up with inquiry about plumbing and electricity. So given the unknowns about communities within the same state, it's no wonder the potential exists to employ false ideas about what life is like for these employees half a world away.]

Perhaps most impactful, though, Flextronics provided faces, an environment, and experiences to recall and appreciate every time I turn on my computer or cell phone.

Like learning the history of a place before I travel there, coming to this factory added a depth to my understanding and an appreciation for the ease with which we attain luxuries today. It's an intricate web of commerce connecting people all over the world; an international infrastructure pooling the talent of inventors, managers, investors, and laborers.

***

Getting Sick in China

Ending my time in Zhuhai on a sour note had a silver lining.

When deciding to go to the hospital to be seen about an illness, I anticipated less-than-ideal conditions, less-than-ideal physicians, and plenty of paperwork. This is the land where kids pee on the sidewalk, litter is dispensed in whatever way is most convenient, and medical professionalism has a different standard than it does back in America. Things in China are a little rough around the edges. Take it or leave it. I thought I'd have to take it one afternoon under Chinese medical care. My friend, Sally, the twenty-eight-year-old office employee of TPR, acted as my guide and interpreter.

We entered the large, multi-storied hospital.

Zhuhai hospital

Once again, inside wasn't the carpeted, homey atmosphere of hospitals and clinics in the United States, but the tiled floors were shiny and the entrance spacious, clean, and new. We filled out a form about a quarter of the size of a full sheet of paper, entering my name, sex, and date of birth. Then we registered me as a walk-in, collected a packet (here comes the paperwork), and paid the registration fee. One must pay up front in China. But the fee was a whopping 5 yuan—less than one dollar.

Sally filled in the cover page, all that was needed (so much for paperwork), and we went upstairs to the directed area: Internal Medicine. Ladies behind some glass waited on us and other patients to give us our room assignment.

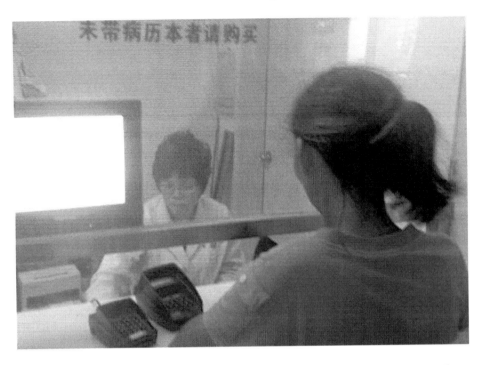

From here we walked to the doctor's office where, in a shocking twist, he was there waiting for *us*. In a matter of fifteen minutes of my first visit, I was being examined.

There's Sally. And my doc.

His examination didn't seem too thorough. I had a sore throat and swollen glands on the sides of my throat/base of my jaw. My muscles ached, and I had a sporadic fever and nausea, consistent headache, my appetite was nil, and I just wanted lots and lots of sleep. "So, Doc, what do you think?" He seemed to ignore most of this, actually, looked in my throat, and ordered a blood test. So we left his room for the area to get this done. But hold on. First you need to pay for that, too. The cost of the blood test: 24 yuan—less than four dollars. Cheaper than the price of a McDonald's meal here.

Down a floor we found the spot for the blood draw: a long counter that resembled bank tellers, each division with slotted glass through which to transact. Replace cash and paperwork with arms and needles and you get the idea.

"Thank you for banking with us."

I stuck my arm inside and she took my deposit. Then Sally and I took the blood vial to the testing area just a few steps away. They took the sample, tested it, and in a matter of a few minutes Sally had the test results in her hands.

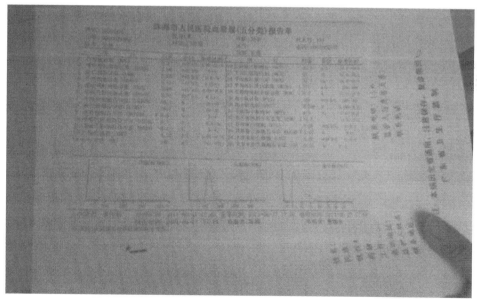

Give it to me in English, Sally.

We then went back to the same doctor, and after examining the results, he prescribed me antibiotics and something for my sore throat. We entered the hospital at 4:55 p.m. and left by 5:35 p.m. Days later, I was feeling fine.

The United States has the best technology and luxury fused into their health care system. But somewhere along the line, it lost some efficiency and a lot of affordability. My visit here sure was a world away from the paperwork, insurance, and multiple visits that a US trip to the doctor requires. There were a lot of things that had me missing home; it was fun and educational to experience aspects here I liked more.

Perhaps just to try it, I should've taken some alternative medicines (though here they probably wouldn't consider it "alternative") which I saw at my neighborhood pharmacy.

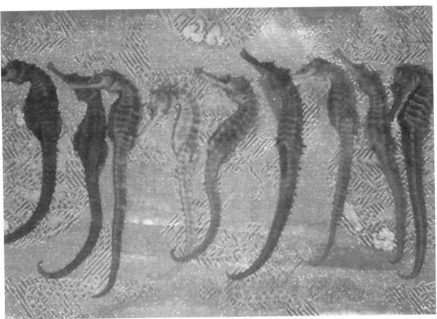

The potion calls for tail of a seahorse...

...and slice of an antler. Grind into a powder, drink with goat's milk, and you're next pregnancy will be twins.

All healthy, I prepared for my final few weeks in China. They would be spent on the road—spanning city, rural hill country, and mountain temples throughout central China. But first, one last meal. The final story of this chapter doesn't have anything to do with institutions, but it did close my year in Zhuhai appropriately.

***

A Closing to My Year with Those Closest to Me

On an evening in June 2011, I dined with seniors: a thin, balding man and his petite, curly-haired wife.

We teachers didn't have our own housing complex. Our school just placed us here and there in various apartment buildings around town: great immersion. And I bet it was somewhat interesting for the residents to have these foreign boys as next-door neighbors. Whenever chance had me and a neighbor walk into the elevator together I didn't have many interactive options. All I could really ever do was pleasantly smile. I came to realize, however, that sometimes a smile is all you need.

Every so often, I'd gain a passing glance at the couple living next door down the hall. Usually, they had with them a couple wee ones who turned out to be their twin boy/girl grandbabies. Usually, all I could ever offer them was a "Ni hao", but by June some language skills accumulated. One day Grandma had Granddaughter in arms pacing the hallway. I broke the ice with a smile; then we continued with a mini-conversation. It capped off with an invitation for dinner at their place a few nights later. I was curious to see how it would unfold given the language, cultural, age, and even dietary bridges we might have to cross, but I'd crossed them before. More than anything I was excited for this intimate slice of life in China.

The night of the dinner, I walked the long journey out my door and twelve paces to the right. Grandmother greeted me with what I can only assume were Chinese "welcomes" and "come-ins." I entered an apartment that was naturally a lot like mine in floor plan, but was homier thanks to a tablecloth, couch slipcover, and shelving with various Chinese decorations. Grandfather was the one in the kitchen. He was really into it, too–head cocked down at a forty-five-degree angle, eyes focused, and feet swiftly shuffling from dining room to kitchen to dining room again.

I sat with the hostess and chatted in broken Chinese. It was tricky. There were things being said the other didn't understand and a few silences filled with Grandpa's kitchen noises. But comfort was comfort, and when you feel welcome you focus on how you *can* communicate: pleasantries, some pantomime, and a phone translator. I discovered they were from Hunan province. I told them about myself—my origins and length of time in China. We talked about the food as the Grandpa delivered it to the table.

Then I looked at the living room floor and noticed two people who've gotten along their whole lives just fine without being able to talk.

Soon, their daughter and son-in-law arrived, and from grandparents to grandchildren three generations of Hunanese Chinese were hosting me for the evening.

With everyone here, it was time to eat. Hunanese cuisine is known for its spiciness, so I had to inquire about some of these dishes. I think they went easy on me this night, though. One pink seaweed salad threw me, but mostly it was beefy, porky, hard-boiled eggy goodness.

Both host families I dined with over the year enjoyed beer (pí jiǔ, 啤酒) *with their meals.*

Despite the added generation and language gaps with this dinner engagement, interaction remained much more familiar than foreign. Grandpa and Grandma encouraged me to keep eating and asked questions about my life in China and in America. They asked that I visit again, but I had to let them know that my time in China was coming to a close.

For dessert, Grandpa took me outside where the sixty-seven-year old offered another example of communicating without speaking.

Via hand gestures and demonstration, I learned the need to swing a forward-tilted paddle in an upward motion.

Look at that! The ball doesn't fly off the table anymore.

My time living in Zhuhai ends right where it began. This was the same table I played on my first morning here.

PART 3: Summer Central China Trek

Chapter Fourteen: Bus, Train, Subway, Plane

For the next three weeks I'd be without the daily grind keeping things (at least somewhat) consistent. Instead, I would have daily doses of fresh sightings and off-the-cuff activities within the perspective-changing places to come. The whole attitude of this travel was a height of exploration and absorption; I was ready to soak it in.

I had some idea of where I'd be going, but only two transports reserved.

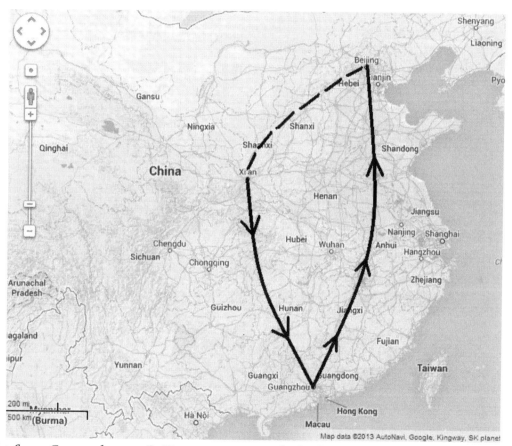

My flight from Guangzhou to Beijing to start; my flight from Xi'an to Guangzhou to finish. In between? We'll see.

Of my 334 days in Asia, this first day of my journey sticks out as providing the best example of transport in China. On my way to Beijing, I'd enjoy the bus, train, subway, plane, and the car of a stranger I met on the plane—in that order. The morning of July 3, 2011, I left my apartment in Zhuhai.

I waited in anticipation at the bus stop with one large suitcase and a stuffed backpack. When I saw the No. 3, I hopped aboard with bulky luggage on the way to the train station. I was full of "expedition presence"—the kind I recalled on that first bus ride to Chicago—knowing that each mile traveled was new earth experienced. This time I was giddy amongst a busload of locals in ordinary commutes to their daily destinations.

I was on my way to the southernmost point of the new high-speed rail being built between Guangzhou and Zhuhai. It wasn't yet complete to my neighborhood, so I needed to take the forty-minute bus ride into the northern skirt of town, a long garment stretching out over the fields of soon-to-be former farmland where, in the middle of openness, sat a parking lot next to the train station. (Today, the rail extends all the way down to Gongbei.) The new train station sat right below the recently assembled elevated rail line supported by massive concrete beams. I walked in, bought my ticket from the lady sitting behind her booth on the ground floor, and then took the escalator up to the rails and saw the train come.

Spacious, comfortable seating awaited me inside the cozy, air-conditioned car. The train glided smoothly along raised path, providing a view of the terrain.

I've shared about China's second-class amenities. Not this train. This was a thrill to ride.

While these sites whizzed by on my right, folks sat to my left.

Somehow I paid a nominal fee for a good distance. It made me look forward (foolishly) to my next train ride on this trip following my time in Beijing.

After just an hour, the train brought me right where I needed to be to descend two flights of escalators—from gliding high above the land to burrowing through it in the Guangzhou subway. Down here I'd have a few more neighbors.

Into the subway system we went, and then into the subway cars we went.

Tunneling through to the airport

At the same airport I had originally arrived to in China, I boarded a plane this day destined for Beijing. On the flight my earphones didn't work, so I couldn't listen to the featured English-language in-flight movie. I turned to the woman to my right to see if my Mandarin could measure up to a conversation. It paid off.

She knew some English and shared that she was a business-owner from Shanghai. Her finely knit brown sweater and white slacks suggested that this woman with medium-length fine black hair and friendly round face was doing well. She asked about my story, and I shared. Then I concluded by asking about transportation into the city. The Beijing airport is a ways outside the city proper, and we landed past midnight so the trains weren't running. My only other option was a pricey taxi. I asked my new friend if she'd like to share one. She said something in broken English about that being okay, her husband coming too. Sure. Sounded good to me. I was saving 100RMB.

We landed, retrieved our bags, and met her son and husband just outside the airport exit. She looked at me while mentioning to her husband something like, "the one on the phone I told you about." If he ever looked back at me it was for the shortest second. I had the feeling he wasn't happy to have me along. I realized as we entered the lighted parking ramp that it wasn't a taxi we were taking, but their own car—the one her husband drove up from Shanghai.

As hospitable as the Chinese were toward Westerners, I was pushing the limits with this guy and stuck between a rock and a hard place—this woman's helping hand and her husband's reasonable annoyance at having to take a stranger to a hostel at 12:30 a.m. somewhere in huge Beijing. Unfortunately, my new friend insisted I sit in the front of their black, shiny sedan while her husband drove and she and their son sat in the back.

When we got onto the highway, the husband asked about directions to my hostel. I wrote them down in pinyin, but he needed the characters. I had a phone number of the hostel (and a dead battery on my phone), so I had to sheepishly ask them to call with their own. He did and got directions for the long ride ahead of us. I tried to make small talk with the husband on the thirty-five-minute ride, but "I don't understand" (wǒ tīng bù dǒng, 我听不懂) was all I got back.

When I wasn't trying to lighten things up in the car, I paid attention to what was outside of it. Through the fog of night I got faint hints that Beijing was looming behind its veil. Each road sign and car and billboard, each exit ramp and bridge along the hedge-lined urban freeway teased me with touches of this legendary city and whole new place for me. I thought back to my first international trip to Guatemala. There also, I was driven a distance from the airport at a late-night hour toward my lodging and absorbing all the newness about me. There, the street lights of this third world city shone off the palm trees, store fronts, gas stations, restaurants, and other traffic. Billboards, all in Spanish, displayed the local beer and cell phone service. Though incredibly different, these two cities were related by the same thrill of my being someplace new, fresh, and accessible.

Suddenly, my mind jolted back into the car as the husband threw on the hazard lights and abruptly pulled over onto the shoulder just shy of an exit ramp. I was confused and assumed car trouble. We stopped, and Mom quickly opened the passenger's side back door. I turned around to see her holding their toddler son just outside the car as he peed on the shoulder of the freeway. It all went down like the pit stop at a NASCAR race. He finished, Mom hoisted him back inside, and off we went—15.4 seconds. Nice job, crew. I assumed this middle-class family would have used diapers.

A little later the husband had to call my hostel again. He got them on the phone and spoke loudly. I think he was frustrated and lost. By now we had exited the freeway system onto city streets and then exited those down alleys just wide enough for the side mirrors to clear (one time we had to pivot them inward to squeak by a dumpster). I felt awkward and tired, but just as I started considering alternative sleeping plans he stopped the car, got out, opened his trunk, and pointed. We were here. Mother refused any money. I hoped they weren't far from their destination. They drove off and from that point on, it was just me and Beijing.

Chapter Fifteen: Highlights from Beijing

On a Day of Worship

Having gotten in late the night before, I spent this Sunday in the way I became accustomed to growing up: taking it easy. I simply wanted to get out and get a feel for this city so central to the history and definition of China. Heavier events would come another day. Interestingly, another element from my childhood Sundays was also demonstrated this day by Beijing: worship.

My hostel was located in a network of narrow alleyways known as hutong (*hútòng*, 胡同). They're an attraction unto themselves due to the history and tradition that has passed through them over the centuries. Buildings and activity filled these tight-knit neighborhoods: small shops; humble, concrete-built homes; and bicyclers pedaling their old contraptions.

Hutong's dwindling presence in Beijing is what fellow Minnesotan, Michael Meyer, wrote about in his book, The Last Days of Old Beijing.

This was from inside a restaurant where I enjoyed inexpensive pork-filled buns on more than one occasion.

Exiting the narrows of my hostel's 'hood, things opened up. A wide, gray-bricked walkway divided two rows of touristy restaurants and kitsch shops.

Exiting this pedestrian passage, I came out just south of the tourist mainstays: Tiananmen Square and the Forbidden City on Qianmen Street.

Streetcars and pedestrians traverse toward the entrance tower to Tiananmen Square, visible in the distance.

I decided to go the other way and visit the appropriate-for-the-Sabbath-named Temple of Heaven or *Tiān tán* (天坛) Park.

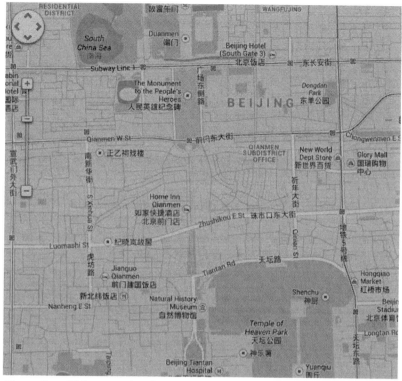

At lower right is Temple of Heaven Park, Tiananmen Square is the gray rectangle in the upper center.

Under blue sky and Beijing warmth, I meandered south into the open, wide roads in this part of town.

Across this final street was the park entrance.

The banner recognizes the 90-year anniversary of the Chinese Communist Part.

Well-known for its structures from Beijing's past, this day Temple of Heaven Park was a hub of social activity in Beijing's present. Right away when I entered, I felt the shine within—not just of the sun—but of dancers moving to a CD of Chinese singing to Western pop beats.

After watching them, I delved deeper into the park. It continued on with lush, thick grass and knotty, old trees. I took to the sidewalks and engaged in some people-watching. I spotted some vendors up where I had turned down some overpriced ice cream when my ears caught the strains of new music further yet into the park. I followed the increasing volume of chords and found that these melodies came not from a radio, but live musicians.

They played the swaying, eerie-calm sounds that typify Chinese music.

After they finished their number, I continued on when yet another set of music-makers nearby reached my ears. This time, the music came from an oratory orchestra. I approached a chorus of over one hundred mainly middle-aged performers singing in celebration.

I don't know what they were singing about, but it felt like a hymn. I enjoyed seeing them transcend to a place of love and joy.

China has much higher rates of atheism than the West; in fact, a whole 60 percent claim to be so. Nonetheless, these folks on this Sunday in this park demonstrated that the need and search for something great and deep exists here despite a recent history and tradition snuffing out religion.

China wasn't always indifferent to religion. After the concert, I shifted attention from live expression to the historic and monumental by walking toward the structures that draw most tourists this way. Leaving the grass and trees, I approached that which gave this park its name.

Hall of Prayer for Good Harvests

Temple of Heaven Park was originally constructed in the early 1400s for emperors from the Ming and Qing dynasties to come and pray for bountiful harvests. Prior to communism, China was much more openly religious. Also back then, this acreage and the structures within weren't for commoners like you and me (unless you have some Chinese emperor blood in you). Only royalty could step foot here.

Imperial Vault of Heaven

Here's what it looks like inside:

Emperors stood on this very floor.

I had heard about Chinese emperors before coming here, but felt no connection to these people, places, and times. They almost seemed otherworldly, perhaps even from a fairytale. I learned this day that they weren't out of this world, just across it, ruling up until the days of my great-great-grandparents, about one hundred years ago.

My park wander was a fitting start to my time in Beijing. Not only did it satisfy and exceed my hopes for a fulfilling Sunday, but it set the stage for further exploration into China's past and present worlds.

***

Tiananmen Square and the Forbidden City

When the emperor wasn't in Temple of Heaven Park praying, he was likely in his "city."

I awoke the next day intent on diving right into the thick of Chinese history (and Chinese tourism). I walked back through my hutong and out to Qianmen Street. But instead of going south and away from Tiananmen Square, I walked toward it. The north/south orientation of it and the Forbidden City meant my route was appropriate—especially because just south of Tiananmen Square were two other picture-worthy structures aligned along this longitude: Arrow Tower and Zheng Yang Gate.

Arrow Tower's north side. Right behind me from this shot was Zheng Yang Gate. The space between them is now a busy roadway; subway lines lie beneath. Modern and ancient intersect all over in Beijing.

Turning around, we have this giant:

North side of Zheng Yang Gate

These two structures by themselves are full of wall-talking history. Like the structures in Temple of Heaven Park, they were initially built in the 1400s—serving as enormous relics from the Ming Dynasty. In 1900, when the West was entrenched in Chinese life, a brief and unsuccessful rebellion against French and British forces took place at these gates. This is known as the Boxer Rebellion.

Turning around and continuing north, I entered Tiananmen Square. I could feel my anticipation rise as I entered this space that was so renowned, yet so foreign. Indeed, it has been a—perhaps *the*—lightning rod of China, a one-hundred-acre urban plain hosting the most grandiose examples of patriotism and the most daunting examples of rebellion versus state authority. This day was typical, with tourists such as these girls demonstrating their support:

Tiananmen Square is also a gauge of the social changes that have taken place over the decades in China and the way these changes overlap today—for example, in the 1950s when it was facelifted in soviet-era styling.

In the 1970s, the Mao Zedong Mausoleum was added in the Square's center.

And when I visited, I saw this large monument recognizing the 90-year anniversary of the Communist Government:

But as much as the famed and unmistakable red-and-yellow hammer/sickle makes this space a sanctuary for the CCP (the cameras in the top left add a nice touch, too), I was also struck by the fact that this was just the latest political attire to clothe the country.

This isn't the best-quality shot, but I like what it says. The two far structures are the Ming-era Arrow Tower and Zheng Yang Gate. The front building is Mao's Mausoleum. There are many layers to China's history; the rise of the Communist government is just the topsoil.

On the north end of Tiananmen Square is the Tiananmen Gate, which featured the famous portrait of Mao as seen below:

Another example of the layering as this façade was built on the existing Ming Dynasty gate.

Viewing all this reminded me of how a commercial space back home can change through the years. Once a restaurant, it then becomes a retail outlet, and finally a bank branch. It's not the buildings themselves as much as the activity and spirit of the people at the time of their occupation that makes the difference.

One can do their homework and identify the Chinese as a communist people with Internet restrictions, a disinterest in religion, and an enthusiasm for their leaders. But those who really do their homework are rewarded with the understanding that "China" is something much bigger: a history, a culture, an ongoing era and a pronounced brand of humanity. Seen in this light, I recognized how "China" actually *uses* the government (rather than vice-versa) as glue, a tool, and an organization. The dynasties and governments have simply decorated "China" in temporary fashion. Whether Taoist, Buddhist, Atheist, Communist, Democratic, or even colonial, China is bigger than any political or social or religious hat.

To observe one such former hat, I entered The Forbidden City.

The Forbidden City was built right along with the Temple of Heaven, Tiananmen Square, the Arrow Tower and Zheng Yang Gate in the early 1400s. This whole complex (980 buildings!) was used exclusively by the emperor and his circle. For five hundred years it was off-limits to anyone else. But when the dynasties fell, the gates opened.

Today it is a busy tourist spot, but it's no trap. This enormous attraction houses an impressive collection of architecture and museums. The above picture is just the "lobby." Walking across it, here is the gate to the city proper:

Once inside, you are offered an actual city's worth of stops.

We only saw a quarter of it in our four-hour visit.

Wait a minute. "We"?

Back at Tiananmen Square I was walking about when a young man approached and asked if he could walk with me and show me around.

His name was Zhong Hua.

I hesitated for a second, wondering if he wanted pay. He assured me he didn't. So I thought, "Why not?" Zhong Hua was great company. He was studying for a summer term in Beijing before going back to his home province, Hubei, where he attended college. He was a proud Christian, helping me—and a couple other tourists I'd introduce him to—simply for the sake of being helpful, he'd declare. We hung out that afternoon taking in the Forbidden City—or at least the quarter of it we covered.

The very chair the emperor sat upon.

The gardens are in the "back," the north end of the complex.

Leaving the Forbidden City on its north end, one faces Jingshan Hill. From the top, a look back affords a view of all that lies within this mystical place.

Like Temple of Heaven Park, here was an area more exclusive and guarded than the White House. Today, though, anyone can meander along as carefree as if it were a town square. I looked at the tourists, descendants of those commoners who toiled in the hillsides and fields centuries ago under the rule of the men who dwelt in this complex. Their ancestors would have been shocked to know their descendants would walk within these walls! This example of history declared to me the massive factors at work directing the sways of social order through time.

One such factor was the father of modern China, and a social sway was demonstrated in Tiananmen Square the following morning.

***

Dead Man Living

I revisited Tiananmen Square—specifically, one structure within it. Doing so revealed a compelling tale of how one person can mean so much to so many.

In the early hours (one needed to wake early for a chance at this attraction) I waited in a line stretching a mile long. No kidding.

Its length stood for this man's legacy; those in line stood for a chance to honor it.

I went to experience the Mao Zedong Mausoleum. Call it a curiosity more than an act of fandom, but several factors compelled me to endure the wait: the fact that his actions birthed modern China; that China's latest chapter continues to be told by the residual effects of his life; that many, many still revere him; and that he was responsible for innumerable deaths. (Though any social movement that changes the fate of a country—let alone one so huge—will involve countless people within a ripe environment, this one man does stand alone as the leader and shaper of Communism's rise in China.)

Frankly, the more I read about the guy, the more impressed I become with a cocktail of respect and disgust. Mao Zedong was a studious young man, but frequently dropped out of school. He read Western works on philosophy and economics. In college he formed student organizations, and after graduating, taught in his home province of Hunan. There, Mao organized political protests in the tumultuous year 1919—when the great line of Chinese emperors had just come to an end due to the rise of Western influence and threats from Japan. In the 1920s, he joined the newly formed Communist party from which he organized peasant movements, land appropriations, and commanded soldiers. By the late 1920s—his mid thirties— he organized his own military force in opposition to the Nationalist government, the Kuomintang (KMT).

Mao was successful in his personal and his party's rise. And perhaps by necessity, he was one cold SOB—killing dissidents, suspected traitors, and enemies (and their wives) along the way. By the time WWII was finished, China was engaged in a civil war pitting the US-backed KMT against Mao's CCP. (A Communist versus Western-backed government has been a sad duality in many third world countries' histories...and presents.) In the fall of 1949, the Communists defeated the Kuomintang by invading and taking over Beijing. The KMT party heads fled to Taiwan where they govern today—and which today remains the controversial island claiming their independence while China claims ownership.

Back on the mainland, though, Mao was the man, and China would change drastically. Mao Zedong initiated sweeping policies, starting with land reforms in which one landlord from every village was ordered to be executed. Counter-revolutionary, capitalist, and political opponent purges led to executions and suicides on a scale beyond belief—hundreds of thousands. The late 1950s began "The Great Leap Forward," a political initiative that put peasants to work on large infrastructure projects and steel production. Though carried out effectively, this was a bad thing. Grain production dipped 15 percent and millions of people died of famine. Mao took a political hit, but came back in the mid-60s doubling-down with his call for a "Cultural Revolution." During this period, anyone tainted with the ways of the West were sent out to the fields to work: professors, educated people, wealthy, etc. What's more, Mao tried to eradicate what he saw as negative aspects of "Old China." This meant the destruction of religious temples—including some buildings of Beishan East-West Cultural Hub, my school's temple property. Under Mao, religion had no place within a system so encompassing.

毛主席給我們的幸福生活

A propaganda poster from the 50s says across the top: "The happy life Chairman Mao gives us."

The Cultural Revolution was the pinnacle of Mao's radicalism, flying in the face of China's hope for progress in the twentieth century. So disastrous, he even ended it early, declaring its finality in 1969. He died in 1976 and the Party, though not as murderously radical, kept the country under a blanket for years after. The ability to choose where to work and live wasn't allowed until the late 70s. I met a woman no older than fifty in Zhuhai during the spring of my year who remembered crying when being told where she was assigned to work following her teacher training in her home province. A lighter consequence was that people weren't allowed to have dogs as pets in Beijing because that was considered capitalistic.

[Sometimes when I saw older folks in China, I thought back to their younger years and how shuttered their world was. When Californians were enjoying the Beach Boys on the coast, and my dad was wrenching on muscle cars in the Midwest and going to the drive-in movies, the Chinese existed in an undeveloped isolate with no choice but to absorb only the art that was authorized by the government. Any person middle-aged and older here must have to pinch themselves when seeing tech-savvy, expressive youth listening to music on their mobile phones.]

Regardless of the improvements since his death, Mao is still modern China's father. He is credited with successfully unifying the country—universalizing schooling and language, and initiating nationwide infrastructure projects. He solidified China's borders that we know today. Women's rights were enhanced as his philosophy taught that all could contribute to the cause. Foot-binding, the practice of breaking girls' feet so they stayed small, was ended. And for many Chinese he offered a sense of identity and hope. When new to China, we English teachers were introduced to TPR staff. One office head introduced herself and her home province with celebration: "I'm from Hunan Province. Same as Chairman Mao!"

At a Mao Zedong-themed restaurant in Zhuhai

Tiffany, my Chinese teacher, did grant that Mao wasn't perfect, but only cut so deep as to refer to The Cultural Revolution as Mao's "mistake." Then there were those who practically worshipped the man.

At the mausoleum, the line snaked around like a balled-up piece of yarn, though shuffled with surprising swiftness. It started north of the mausoleum and headed south along its side.

We were on the left. On the right were those on the way back.

It wasn't just a simple to and fro. There was a huge loop we had to make before heading back north.

Then, once we got back on the north side, we turned left to finally face the finish line.

This was just the final stretch.

Just before making it to the steps, there were tables with white roses for sale.

Many people purchased roses, but I chose to be a conscientious observer this day.

The line parted when nearing the building: right and left—and thus you stay as you walk through the building. This day I was a lefty; I ascended the stairs. No pictures—no cameras. (They didn't even let you enter the line with one. All these photos were taken with my phone.) Passports were said to be required. I showed mine to a guard right before entering the Mausoleum, but I saw other Westerners get in without theirs. They also reminded visitors of no talking. Fine with me—I didn't have much to say, but I did have things to write. And despite some protestation from my hostel manager—they thought that wouldn't be allowed, either—I brought along a pen and paper to note what I saw inside.

I entered the stone-walled structure into an openness of white floors, 30-foot-tall ceilings, auditory echoes, and a visual formality that resembled a capitol building or cathedral. In a further mixture of these two, a half-Christ/half-Lincoln, enormous white statue of a seated

Chairman Mao sat elevated forty feet before us. Behind him was a giant panorama of a mountainous landscape, offering a visual perspective of the Chairman's greatness. With proud expression, he looked over our heads. At his feet were two tables, one for each line and each covered with those white roses all laid uniformly into mounds. This was the one deviation allowed on the tour: to humbly walk up toward the Chairman, bow, and set a flower on the pile. Many did. Bright red carpets marked our way, directing each line to either side door around the statue and through the back wall. I took the red-carpet treatment out the left-hand door.

Past the threshold and into the next room, another vision of the Chairman greeted us; this one saw him on his back with eyes closed. His corpse lay embalmed thirty-five years from death in a clear casket elevated on a five-foot-tall foundation. His face was peaceful; his body was draped with the Chinese flag. I took in the surreal sight only briefly as necessitated by officials who kept the line moving. Walking past the Chairman in the flesh, I exited out the other side of the building, having been inside the mausoleum for maybe four or five minutes.

From the hero to the human, I next got to know life on the streets of Beijing.

***

Beijing Means Business

People back in Zhuhai had a way of fitting into the nooks and crannies of commercial opportunity. But here in Beijing, I saw salespeople in places even "nookier" and "crannier." In the hot July sun, several folks simply stood around tourist areas with a box of popsicles—one yuan a piece. Down in the cracks of the commercial fabric of Beijing, these popsicle peddlers were naturally hard to stop. But efforts were ramped up considerably compared to Zhuhai, and when officers came by, the popsicle people fled. One was caught cold-handed, the guard sticking his hand in his box and crushing the merchandise. No fines, just squish.

For those whose products were more valuable and less portable, the threat of police was more serious.

I sought the help of Zhong Hua to find the Beijing Wal-Mart. I was curious to see what a Wal-Mart looked like in China, plus I wanted to get some Western snacks. Getting off the subway in an industrial/retail area of Beijing, we crossed a pedestrian overpass above a highway. Down the steps on the other side, we encountered a group of five or six vendors and twice as many shoppers tucked alongside and under these stairs. These folks literally found their nook to do business.

One woman just had a bunch of socks laid out on a blanket, and it so happened I needed some so I took a look. I was just starting to examine when suddenly Sock Lady swiftly reached across the display, bundled up her blanket of goods, and got ready to bolt. (Evidently, she had done this before as it was all gathered in about 1.5 seconds.) However, almost as quickly, she calmed down.

This street merchant thought the police were on their way, ready to confiscate her humble, unlicensed inventory. But no worries; false alarm. However, alarms were probably never really off. I heard police had plainclothes officers mingling around for surreptitious infiltration into these "commercial zones." For now, though, Sock Lady redisplayed her merchandise.

Next to her, a mother and son had a picnic blanket bookstore.

Through Zhong Hua, I asked her why she led this lifestyle on the street, always having to lookout for the police. Couldn't she just get a job at the nearby Wal-Mart?

Visible from their sales nook

She responded that she didn't reside here in Beijing, but another province; she lived here only for the summer. Her boy was off of school now (July), and she needed to watch him while maintaining some kind of income. So they made their way here where a person with time, bargaining skills—and quick feet, if need be—could make a yuan. In the fall they go back home, the boy goes to school, and the mom goes to her regular job. I wanted to help out, so I re-examined her books and found a good one to buy. As for the Sock Lady, I wanted to do a little comparison shopping first—so I went to that Wal-Mart.

Having been in China over ten months by now, I longed for my favorite Western snacks and anticipated this visit with visions of trail mix and beef jerky dancing in my head. Looking back, I'm not sure why—ten months was long enough to know better. But because of these high hopes, my spirits were soured when, instead of trail mix I found shrink-wrapped peanuts (which I often found stale), and instead of beef jerky I found shrink-wrapped chicken's feet.

Speaking of "visions dancing in their heads," though, I did find one notable and unmistakable sign of American culture seen below:

I can't imagine many Chinese folks relating to a story about a blonde-haired, blue-eyed boy celebrating a Christian holiday with the dream of gun ownership. Nevertheless...

I also anticipated cheap socks. I figured if US Wal-Mart prices were cheaper, then the prices here were going to be crazy low. But I found that, similar to fast food prices, socks at Wal-Mart actually mimicked American rates—despite probably being made here. It seemed a no-brainer, then, to go back and get them from the Sock Lady outside. However, I was struck by the predicament that Wal-Mart versus Sock Lady prompted for the moral-minded consumer. At home, many people say that it is best to support the independent business community and combat Wal-Mart's alleged unfair and unethical practices. However, on the streets of Beijing these mom-and-pop operations were illegal. They didn't pay licenses, and they sold products with pirated name-brand logos. Buying at Wal-Mart, on the other hand, would help a developing country by supporting "legitimate" business that pay taxes for city infrastructure.

I bought from the Sock Lady. Hers were half the price—though probably had half the quality.

The next day I jetted to see the other side of the business world—Beijing's Central Business District (CBD) or *Běijīng Shāngwù Zhōngxīn Qū* (北京商务中心区).

I popped out of the subway system among the clean streets, newly-built skyscrapers, wide sidewalks, green grass, and Starbucks. I enjoyed the aesthetic clash from my hostel's rugged surrounding. When walking a particular couple blocks between towers, I noticed the human clash, too. All these well-dressed folks were going about their day—swiftly. Watching them, I started to feel a bit outclassed and also saw how the culture of business heightens and perpetuates everyone's "business" look: the game faces on their speed-walking bodies that say, "I'm on my way to someplace important." Accentuating the impersonal touch, many conversed on cell phones.

[It occurred to me that productivity, demands, and the one-upmanship of the urban business world programs people into a focused, task-oriented manner. There's no drill sergeant, but I got to thinking that seeing someone with a smile on his face here would almost look as silly as a marine with his eyes crossed and tongue sticking out. It must take quite the incredible person to live in any "tough" business environment and maintain one's interpersonal warmth. Taking the time to say hello to strangers, or even smile, might distract from the mission at hand. It's no wonder that business is criticized for putting profits before people. It's hard to do both.]

This oblivious-to-others nature I observed in Beijing's CBD had me appreciating the friendly, personable environs of Blackduck—or, since I was in Beijing, my hostel's hutong offering pork buns for sale on the corner and middle-aged guys so relaxed they don't even bother putting on a shirt.

This desire for the informal made the next stop on my trek quite appropriate.

Later this day, I went with Zhong Hua to the train station. While I had known where my next stop would be, I hadn't yet figured out when it would be. Zhong Hua spoke to the teller standing behind the glass divider to help me buy a ticket for the following night. I felt okay about purchasing a seat ticket as opposed to a bed. Sure, I acknowledged sitting would make a tougher overnight ride, but I've slept in airplanes before. Plus, I really enjoyed my seated train ride from Zhuhai to Guangzhou. After I bought the ticket, we walked back to my hostel where I thanked Zhong Hua for his services and friendship and said goodbye.

The following afternoon, I packed all my things and readied for my train ride out that night.

Chapter Sixteen: To Rural China

Though this next leg of my journey belonged to the same body that was this trek, it would have been difficult to find a more opposing experience to the official, touristy, metropolitan environs of Beijing as I did here in rural Henan province.

The attraction that brought me here? An elderly woman.

***

Chinese Choo-Choo

I was excited about this 415 mile-(668 km) train trip from Beijing to Ruzhou.

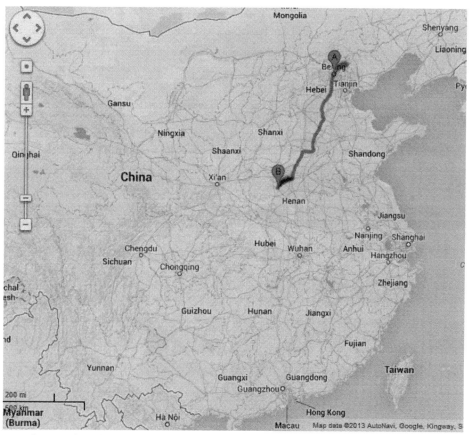

I imagined the miles and miles of terrain to take in, gliding through a field or soaring through and around mountains.

At 8 p.m. I arrived at the West Train Station in Beijing—a large, open, airplane terminal-like building.

Big electronic signs hung high in this expansive room, keeping travelers' eyes looking up at the gate numbers and travel times for their rides. I read my gate and rolled my things to a large room with lots of bench seating. I waited here for several minutes before they announced our train. When they did so, a hoard of travelers stood with me to line up at the ticket-taker counter. Eventually, I gave the attendant my ticket, passed through one of those rotating, waist-high metal tri-bars (those things were always a pain with rolling luggage), and then exited the building behind the counter.

Along with the other travelers, shuffled toward the train along the railway platform. It reminded me of what train stations looked like on old movies minus all the steam. I walked along the train until I found my car and stepped up inside. Unlike the comfortable cabins I'd seen in film, however, and certainly unlike my train ride earlier, I discovered a situation where there were many more people than seats.

Where's everyone going to sit?

Suddenly, the memories of what I'd heard about China train travel resurfaced from their dormant state, having been lulled by my previous relaxing ride. As I stepped into the aisle, I found an answer to the seat dilemma.

Seeing this man, I had another recollection: the woman I saw just moments earlier standing out on the platform holding up small collapsible stools for sale. Perhaps this guy would like one.

All the tight moving about in this small space caused me some dread. I foresaw and fore*felt* the restlessness of a ten-hour, overnight ride. At least I had a seat. The right side of the car had sets of two-by-two seat benches facing each other with a tabletop in the middle, connected to the side of the car. To sleep, these riders could either try to lean back on the erect seats like in an airplane or they could try to lean down on the table top, their arms or bags as pillows. They were the lucky ones—the other side of the aisle had seat-groups of three-by-three facing each other. I got one of these, and on my particular bench I was the monkey in the middle. Still, it was better than the aisle seat, because the table top extended out only so far, leaving this person with nothing to lean forward upon to sleep. The twenty-something guy to my right in this predicament chose to kneel on the floor and rest his head against the seat bottom. And yet still we were the lucky ones because there were those in the car who had no seat at all. It's better than no ticket, but these poor folks either stood in the aisle, sat on their bags or on the floor, or picked up a makeshift stool from the lady back at the station—and then deal with passersby in the aisle all night long.

After getting my luggage stored above, I put my backpack between my legs and snuggled into place. Soon, the train started to move, adding another contrast from my previous ride via its shaky ground-level experience. One constant, though, was a benefit that public transport provided all year: meeting people. I started off my time on the train by observing the fellow passengers, each with their own destination and story.

These guys sat across from me. The gentleman on the right was returning to his home province while on holiday from work.

She was returning home from college.

Next is a picture of my lucky bench-mates:

When in transport with others, we have the chance to learn about the places they go, the stories they tell, and the reasons for their travel. The web of roadways, railroads, waterways, and flight routes tether our lives together, each strand a point A to B and a story at either end to be unraveled by the inquisitor.

We journeyed all through the night with the intimacy of strangers, necessitating a "roughing it" transport mentality that made a forty-five-minute standing ride on a Zhuhai bus seem fun. An arrhythmic knocking of the train wheels over the tracks was our beat. Our "dance" was random, stuttering upper-body, back-and-forth sway-jerks. Lights remained on in car the whole night. No matter, I eventually was exhausted enough to manage some sleep—hour-long intervals here and there using my backpack as a pillow on the table top. The night was a blur, confusing my recollection of what occurred between the frequent stops and my short sleeps: a guy smoking in one fuzzy memory, a woman breastfeeding in another.

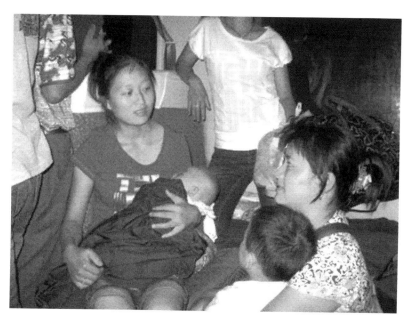

Eventually, morning came. I met it with the surreal quality that a lack of sleep provides—a realization that the day has begun, a gratitude that the night is over, and a half-alertness along with some discomfort that prevents full appreciation.

"Zǎo shang hǎo" (早上好), which is Mandarin for "Good morning."

[Later in this trek I'd have some hindsight gratitude when a couple Austrian women shared their rough ride with me. Their car was so crowded that passengers on the floor curled up at their feet, using the women's back-packs as pillows.]

At around 7 a.m. Saturday, July 9, we arrived at my station. This destination would serve up the most stunning example of hospitality and most insightful eating experience, because the family I stayed with owned a restaurant. Also, it was here I'd reenter the charm of small-town living, and most important, meet that special old woman for whom I'd traveled all this way.

***

Good Ol' Down-Home Hospitality

My train stopped in the city Ruzhou, but my destination was actually a town just outside it called Ruyang.

It was one of those times you witness the day's first light but your body says you ought to be asleep. I hopped off the train car and awkwardly wheeled my suitcase over the dirt and track to get to the station platform.

Hanging a left on the platform up ahead, I greeted the town and my hosts.

My former student, June, set this all up. If you recall, in March I asked her in class if I could visit her grandmother: the ninety-nine-year-old with the small, bound feet. The twenty-six-year-old agreed, though with some bewilderment. Of course this was in March, and I didn't plan on making my voyage until July. So I suppose it was easy for June to go along with the idea for the time being. As summer neared, however, she started to tell me it would be very hard for me to find her grandmother and that there was nothing to do in this part of China. Regardless of how much of this was true and how much was June's revealed lack of interest, I didn't blame her. She would have to arrange it as the translator. And putting the shoe on the other foot, I don't know how I'd feel burdening my family with my language teacher's interest in my grandmother's feet. As it turned out, though, beyond June's hesitation was a very willing family. And when they expressed excitement for their first American visitor, she was then pleased to help arrange my visit.

I didn't know how I'd recognize them, but of course they had no problem recognizing me. June's brother-in-law, his toddler daughter (June's niece), and June's little brother all greeted my arrival at the station. Brother-in-law walked up with a smile. He had a medium build, a friendly, broad face, and would take me under his wing during my time here. June's brother was a bit shorter with boyish looks. The toddler was adorable with what I considered to be interestingly short hair.

Brother-in-law with daughter

Leaving the station, we got into Brother-in-law's van and drove twenty minutes to Ruyang.

Here in small-town China, center lines are treated as suggestions.

Ruyang had a few thousand people and a "dusty" feel along its main street. This main drag was lined with six-story buildings—most of which, with their weathered walls, looked to be built thirty years ago.

Ruyang, Henan Province

Brother-in-law and his wife, June's sister, owned a restaurant here. It was squeezed right in along main street and offered me the extra chance to take in the local home cooking. We went there first thing; they wanted to feed me. Inside was a simple, one-room dining space with a kitchen in the back. Again, we had the smooth, off-white tiled floors and white walls. It had ten or so plain but well-built wooden tables and chairs. Each table had a burner in the center with which to keep the fish—the staple entrée—steamy warm. The walls had blown-up menus pasted upon them. There was a fish tank immediately to the right as you entered and a display counter further along the right wall with all the side dishes behind glass. The cash register was at the back of the room, and behind it, another display, this one of alcohols to purchase.

Although I was dragging from the overnight ride, June's family was nonetheless eager to offer me their ethnic eats for lunch. They led me to the food display to take my pick. There was a plate of diced egg whites coated in oil, a pile of purplish noodles, some brown seaweed, an attractive plate of sliced cucumbers and about six other offerings. I chose the eggs and cucumbers; they threw in the others I mentioned, and they centered it all with a fresh fish.

The children—the toddler daughter and another brother/sister cousin combo—sat down with me at the table nearest the register. A few minutes after sitting, mounds of food were piled before us.

Oh, the light, flakey, crunchy, salty, sweet, tender, juicy food in China!

After lunch, Brother-in-Law walked me to my hotel that they evidently paid for or arranged in some fashion. It was only two blocks away on the same side of the street and, like the restaurant, squeezed within many adjacent businesses along this main road.

The lobby had the typical white floors and walls. I was pleasantly surprised that the woman at the front desk knew English—the only person I met here who did. Another surprise was that through the lobby the hotel morphed into what seemed to be an entirely new building. Minus the sterile feel out front, the dated carpeting in the halls, soft-colored walls, and heavy wooden doors gave this cozy dwelling the feeling of a US hotel circa 1973. My room echoed the style, including worn furniture and saggy bed. But I flopped down and enjoyed a much needed afternoon nap following the long, restless train ride.

Zzzzzzzzzz.

I awoke hours later to some door rapping. I overslept my nap and was expected back at the restaurant. I hopped out of bed, got ready in a jiff, and Brother-in-law and I walked back out of the hotel as evening approached. A small town Saturday night was upon us, and outsider or not, the feel of a rural community enjoying themselves following the week of work was unmistakably familiar.

Right away I was offered dinner. This time, though, I watched the meal prep. They first netted a fish fresh from that tank just inside the door. And more than just the capture being demonstrated right before my eyes, they also took the black, wiggly, seven-pound catch and proceeded—with some real violence—to club it on the head with a wooden mallet so it would not flop around as they carried it to the kitchen. At least you knew it wasn't filleted alive.

I followed the angler and his catch into the kitchen back behind the counter. Through a plastic-draped door I saw stainless steel sinks, cluttered countertops, a blackened range and nearby walls, and a dirty, tiled floor. Two strapping young cooks, along with Brother-in-law, handled their kitchen business as if it was second nature. One cook had his shirt half-way undone; the other liked to smoke while cooking. It was a raw cooking experience.

The smells and sounds of preparation whetted my appetite. And thirty minutes later, I was enjoying the fruits of their labor.

As I sat eating, the local dinner rush started coming through the front door. A group of five men lumbered in, carrying themselves without a care in the world and requesting food like they owned the place—not in an arrogant way, but with warm familiarity. Somehow, it brought me back to my days in high school.

[I remembered the same total ease and comfort with which I moved through the halls of Blackduck High School. I saw no need then to be self-conscious the way one does in the company of strangers—for there really weren't any. Having no ambiguity amongst my peers comforted me. I then contrasted this with living in a city. It's not debilitating, but still, in Minneapolis I walk about in public and familiar with practically no one around me, unless coincidence crosses my path with an acquaintance. In these urban settings, I (I think we) rely more on the social scripts for how to act in a grocery store, in traffic, on the street, which just isn't as natural, nor as genuine. It's at least necessary to create a mode of indifference to the many people in urban life. To me, this indifference opposes openness.]

At this restaurant in Ruyang I then thought, "Gosh, maybe I'm a small-town boy after all." Having lived eighteen years in tiny Blackduck, Minnesota, I was a little surprised that it took being in Ruyang, China, to help me realize the charms of small-town life. And it all started with that group of lumberers—who, with their aggressive mannerisms and interaction, and even their clothing, hair, and "church-like" conservative appearance—reminded me remarkably of my mother's cousins.

Later that night I left the restaurant to walk the dark, empty streets. It was clear black, stars glittering, and I realized I missed that aspect of small-town living, too. A few young, out-late locals approached and looked at me. One said "hello" and giggled. I then turned a corner on this comfortable summer evening and saw Ruyang's own outdoor barbeque.

Almost everyone had a one-liter glass bottle of beer, and I actually encountered my first drunken Chinese person. The young man was trying so hard to speak English to me, which can be difficult even for the sober Chinese or drunken American to do.

The next morning Brother-in-law took me to breakfast. This time it was a small-town Sunday morning at a no-frills style of eatery that exists in towns across China: a few tables and food preparation set up on the sidewalk.

Ma and Pa Kettle

Brother-in-law ordered for me, and we sat down next to some other area eaters.

Biscuits with green vegetable baked in

The food was new to me and pleasantly comforting—as were my seat neighbors who were so open and welcoming.

It revealed that the first meal of the day can put a little extra spring in one's step when it's a shared experience.

Beyond even what I knew growing up, small-town China possessed a new level of openness.

***

Growing up in Old China: Bone-Breaking Pressure

In China around 1000 years ago, a unique trend began in the area of fashion, custom, and gender. Parents started to tightly wrap the feet of their young daughters so the feet wouldn't grow large. This binding became extreme enough to require the breaking of the toes and of the arch, and it evolved to become a common practice throughout all the classes of Chinese society for hundreds of years. This practice hasn't taken place for some time now. The society it represented was much different than the one we see in China today. But it wasn't that long ago–phased out in the 1930s and 40s–and the fact that things were so different just some decades ago speaks to how much change has taken place here. I think that's what intrigued me about the practice of xiao jiao (xiǎo jiǎo, 小脚) "small feet" and the women who have them. It is a marker of this change and represents the actions people take under the weight of social order.

After breakfast that Sunday morning, Brother-in-law, his toddler daughter, and June's mother took me to see the woman I'd traveled so far and waited months to meet. We stood alongside the wide, empty main street in Ruyang. Soon, a small bus slowed, and in we went.

Grandma lived outside of town—outside of asphalt roads, as a matter of fact.

After several miles of town and country, hills and fields, we stopped at a stretch amongst a few residences. Now it was time to walk a mile or two.

To see the woman with bound feet, we now had to use ours.

We passed by animal...

...neighbor...

...and landscape.

Tobacco

The asphalt ended and became a dirt path. Then our sunny, Sunday stroll started to slope downward and off to the right, stopping at a few buildings at the bottom.

It was a farmstead—a compound housing family and extended family. One such member met us at the entrance.

The queen bee of this hive stayed in perhaps the most humble brick/mud building of them all.

Brother-in-law showed the way inside.

"Yeah, so we got this American guy out there who wants to check out your feet. You, uh, cool with that, Grandma?"

She expected me, and I entered. I first just surveyed her humble home.

Corn cobs

Then I watched the family interact.

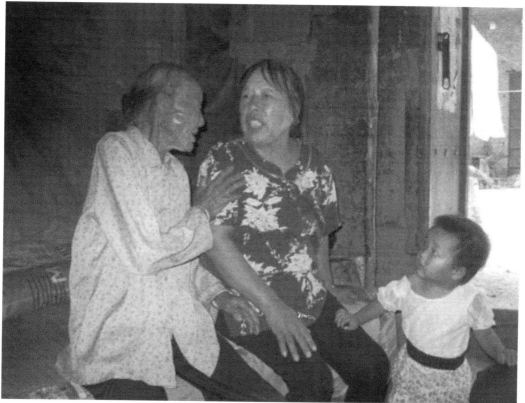

Three of four generations of women, with the third generation, June's sister, back in Ruyang running the restaurant.

And with the help of my friend Jerry on speaker phone, we began to talk.

Her name was Jing Yuan, a ninety-nine-year-old who's lived around these parts her whole life. When she was six, her feet were prepared for the binding process. From what she described and from what I've read, this meant stretching wet bandages around her little feet and wrapping her toes down and in. Eventually, the arch of the foot is pressured to break upward. It's that tight. Jing Yuan did say that the pain wasn't too bad if she didn't move her feet. Unfortunately, this was necessary as girls had to walk on them to secure the shape. For Jing Yuan, this was ninety-three years ago.

I took her foot on my lap and removed the sock.

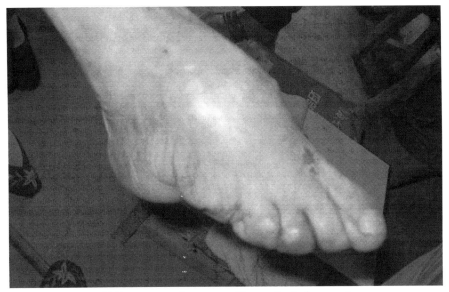

Where are the toenails and pinky toe?

Once the shape was set, the bindings would stay on—for good. It consumed a big portion of a woman's day changing the bandages and washing—crucial, too, as some girls died from infection. As you can see, Jing Yuan doesn't have hers bound any longer.

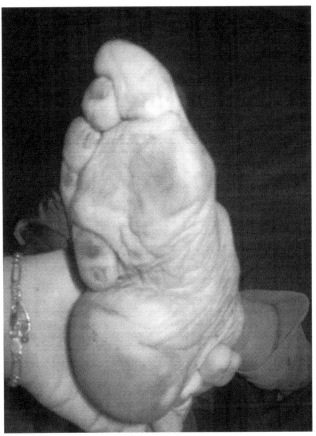

We see or hear about these kinds of customs throughout the world. I always wonder how they start. Historians believe the ancient wealthy in China wanted to emulate the small feet of some dancers of the day.

I don't how it came to breaking girls' feet. What I *can* understand is how this trend could perpetuate and be maintained. Like many trends, foot-binding began in the upper class and trickled downward. (In America the same thing happens with baby names.) Foot-binding became a symbol of wealth, of not needing to do manual work. And somewhere along the line it became sexy. So like a poor woman today with a knock-off Prada bag, the lower classes followed suit. This was really tough, though, because unlike the upper-class women, the poor did need to work. Jing said she remembers being a young woman and working outside in the garden with a cane. Nonetheless, poor people bound their girls' feet anyway, because if your girl had feet twice the size of the others, then she would have no place in her world.

By seeing how Jing's life was shaped by her culture, I could apply that perspective to see the ways all individuals are directed by the ways of their people. Hair, clothing, circumcision, tattoos. Whatever the custom, the people involved may define themselves and others based on such parameters. And when involved, it can be hard to imagine a life outside of it, but it's enlightening to do so and to see that sometimes the definitions we give on account of such behaviors are superficial.

It's freeing—unlike this tradition.

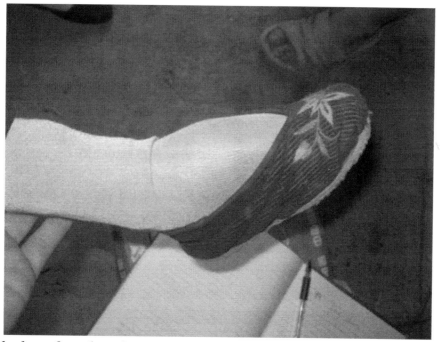

It wasn't the bare foot that the men liked, but the visual of the small feet in their shoes.

As a relic of the past and a symbol for change, what was once seen as practically mandatory is now looked back on with interest and curiosity at best and with disgust and embarrassment at worst. In a complete turnaround, the wealth and status exemplified by a woman's bound feet was then frowned upon and eliminated by the communist mentality and order that praised labor. (I'd regularly see women working on a building demolition or road construction in China.)

Laborer in Zhuhai

As a result of the political and social shifts, Jing Yuan practiced foot binding for "only" fifty years. She said taking the bandages off for good was also painful. The foot wants to adjust to its new freedom, though she said her feet didn't change back all too much.

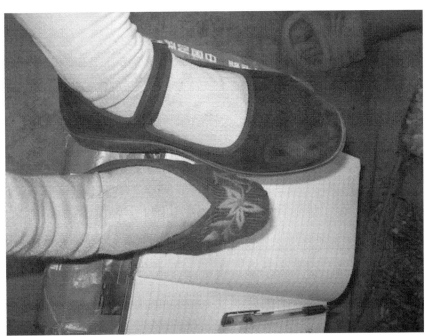

Jing's foot below and her daughter's above

Some ladies of Jing's day couldn't walk and needed to be carried. But Jing Yuan could—then and now. We went outside where she mingled with her progeny.

The matriarch of the farmstead

As a child, her whole world was defined by the order that shaped her feet. Now these feet clash with the same world she endured so much pain to fit into. The society—the trends, customs, and behaviors that her generation of Chinese defined their lives by, the whole aura of those days, where did the times go that required her feet to be bound? They're gone.

Lesson learned: Don't get too bound up in the social pressures of your day.

Brother-in-law, his daughter, June's mom, and I walked back up the road and rode the bus back to Ruyang. The next morning, June's little brother dropped me off at the train station in Ruzhou.

***

A couple weeks before I left Zhuhai for this trek, it was I who went to June with cold feet about this crazy idea to travel to a desolate part of China and burden a strange family just to see an old lady. By then, though, it was June assuring me it would be okay. She was right, and her family made it so.

June's brother

At the train station, I bought my ticket and awaited my transport with all the other travelers.

Off to other adventures

Chapter Seventeen: Martial Arts and Meditative Craft

Chinese Choo-Choo 2

While in Ruyang I narrowed down my next destination to one of two options: I could travel to northern Henan province to sightsee the Longmen Caves (lóngmén shíkū, 龙门石窟), where centuries ago Buddhist monks decorated the interiors with a museum of sculptures; or, I could head south into the adjacent province of Hubei. I had read about a beautiful mountain there with an abundance of history itself: Wǔ dāng Shān (武当山). Shān (山) means mountain, and atop it was the birthplace of the slow, rhythmic martial art, tai chi.

Between the two it was a mental coin flip of educational opportunities. But I recall thinking quite vividly, "I can go see the art and caves and learn how monks lived. Or I can go one step beyond and actually live as other ancients did by practicing a meditative martial art."

I hopped aboard the train at the Ruzhou Station for Wu Dang Shan located in the northwest part of Hubei Province.

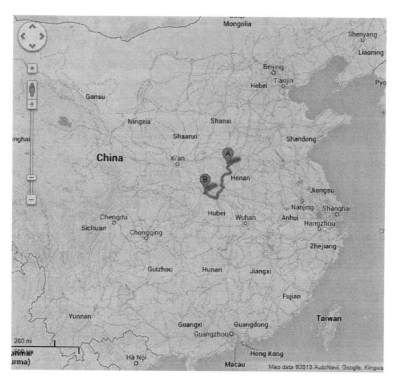

I talked earlier about the "lucky ones" traveling in my seated train car to Ruzhou, but it was the folks in the sleeper cars who were quite better off. (And I guess we don't have to stop here when comparing. Plenty travelers opt out of trains altogether and pay a few extra yuan for a plane ticket...where we have a whole new tier of travel classes.) In these trains, though, it was night-

and-day how the mood changed when I splurged for a sleeper on this train ride to Wu Dang Shan. My previous ride had a gravity to it, a "we gotta get through this" attitude filling the air. In this car, things were chipper. Money doesn't buy happiness, but the comfort gained sure helps.

The beds were three-high with six in a compartment facing each other. Our car had about eight compartments. Along the feet of the beds ran the narrow walkway to make your way about the car. A covey of kids near my bed played games with one another throughout our daytrip. And typical of children, they were either afraid to speak up or hadn't a sliver of fear in them.

These fell into the latter category.

They got a kick out of the white guy on board. They wanted to speak with me, and one sweet boy gave me a few seashells he had collected.

Again, public travel allowed access into people's lives and hearts.

***

Up the Mountain, in the Now

I prepared to depart the train as it slowed for the Wu Dang Shan station. A couple adult passengers had indicated to me that this was where I needed to get off. I hopped onto the platform that summer afternoon and was immediately uncertain of my decision to leave the train since I was the only one to do so at what I thought would be a popular destination. Also, the happening downtown atmosphere described in my guidebook was nowhere to be found. Finally, I had to ask, "Where is the 'shan'?" It was the only time on my travels that I felt truly alone—and nervous. "Did I get off at the wrong stop?" I thought.

I stared at the train chugging away in the distance. A security guard keeping watch for who-knows-who was my only companion.

I missed the crowds reliably found at train stations to help me know the direction to go next.

I went down the platform stairwell lugging my stuffed suitcase in that leaning, swaying way you have to carry something heavy in one arm. I longed for the urban convenience of a luggage ramp. The station exit led to a parking lot overlooking "town." There were only a few small, shoddy stores and restaurants along the small street that ran downhill from the station parking lot to the highway below. In that parking lot, a young man approached and aggressively offered me a ride. "Wu Dang Shan," I said, stressing the "shan." He nodded, which I liked, but offered a price that I didn't. It was so high that I couldn't go with him despite his knocking the price down 50 percent as I walked away. I saw a half-sized bus parked in the lot. It read "Wu Dang Shan" on its side. That looked promising. I inquired to the driver, who nodded with approval. I boarded, and when a couple other Chinese folks hopped on, we headed into town.

It turned out the train station was moved outside of town a few years back. This explained the lack of mountain. And the little outcrop of stores and shops seemed to be merely an accompaniment to the new station location. Indeed, it was a good twenty minutes until I got into town. But once we got there, I knew I was in the right place.

Wu Dang Shan, a quaint and energetic town

Now I just needed to find a place to stay. I rolled my suitcase along bumpy, bricked sidewalks looking for a hostel.

Wu Dang Shan has tourism appeal, so I spied many hotels. But I wanted a hostel, so I kept on block after block. Soon, a friendly-looking middle-aged woman motioned me emphatically to follow her. Something about her seemed trustworthy. She led me two blocks away to a set of dusty, concrete steps up a six-story apartment building. On the second floor she opened a door to reveal a cozy little guest home. It belonged to her and her husband, an apartment that they reconditioned into a mini-motel. I got a pint-sized room for sixty yuan, and it was perfect. Another mom/daughter combo booked the other room in this apartment.

Mother/daughter on the left; establishment owner on the right

With my basic needs met, I was able to step upon this platform of comfort and reach for the higher needs of my time here: learning tai chi up the mountain. I found a couple schools online and got ahold of one with an English-speaking employee. The next morning, a trainer from the school knocked on the apartment/hotel door and took me away.

Before we ascended, he walked me into the thick of Wu Dang Shan town center to a small establishment selling martial arts outfits. I didn't anticipate this expense, but when in Rome.

Okay. Now we were ready to head up the mountain.

Next we took a taxi the "base camp," the area where we paid admission and hopped aboard a bus to the school.

Following him to pay for ticket

After getting passes, we rode up. It started to get gorgeous.

I just had to hold on to my seat between photo opportunities due to tight lefts and sharp rights curving up Wu Dang Shan.

After several minutes the bus slowed and my trainer pointed out the door. We were here.

Follow him into the cabin

Opposite the cabin and across the road was a breathtaking view of deep green valleys and distant peaks. I was impressed by the vastness, by the height of these peaks. The temperature indicated the elevation as well. The town was hot, but up here was cool. I walked to the cabin.

My trainer pointed me to my room, and I wandered around a couple minutes getting to know the place. The conditions and the way of life, I'd learn, were almost as much a part of the practice as the martial arts performance. To the left of the front door were my quarters.

I had this room to myself for a few days. After that, I was paired with another guy from Chongqing.

Straight in through the front door of our cabin was the commons/dining area.

Then through here and to the right, was the kitchen. It wasn't the cleanest, but certainly not the dirtiest I had seen in China.

Hanging back in the upper right are sides of bacon next to feathered ducks. On the floor to the left is a large wok set atop a wood burning oven.

I didn't photograph the bathroom, but I will report with warm memories that a water heater was present. My fellow students were two boys around ten years old, a few men in their twenties and thirties, two young female students ages twelve and nineteen, and a group of adult women who took things a little less seriously. There were three or four trainers. All were Chinese.

I arranged a four-day, three-night stay—not long, but still, I figured a day full of tai chi is a long day and would challenge me. My trainer, not wasting any time, took me right back outside after I dropped my things off in my room.

I followed my trainer across the street to the concrete platform where we'd practice.

He set down his bag and started to demonstrate, just he and I that midmorning. I have to say, I was a little unnerved about starting. "Uh, can't we start this after lunch?" I remember thinking. I rediscovered the truism: *Easier said than done.*

This was his choreography: slowly step to the right with your right foot while raising your arms straight out. As your left foot does its symmetrical move to the left, your arms sway in that direction while settling into a fighting position with loose fists. After just a moment, your fighting pose morphs into arms straight out again—this time still facing the left. Then when your right foot starts its step, you sway your arms back to the right.

Repeat, repeat, repeat.

Tai chi (tài jí quán, 太极拳, means "supreme ultimate fist") is the martial art of mimicking fighting maneuvers only slowed way down.

Getting started, I realized this was another endeavor in life that learned people make look easy. Tai chi was an immediate mental challenge because it brought me face to face with my tendency for my mind to wander. Other martial arts may have appeased me with quick, distracting movements, satisfying a short attention span—but not tai chi. Its gradual, repetitive nature made it both tempting for a bored mind to drift off but necessary that it stay focused lest you disturb the routine. You have to observe your slow, smooth movement as would a cat looking over a mouse hole. On top of all this, doing some of these movements was almost as physically awkward as doing the feminine dance moves in the fall.

I was doing things a little backward at first. You just have to slowly, gradually, smoothly keep...screwing up. And when you do, you do it again, and again, and again. And when you do it right, you do it again, and again, and again.

While practicing this first morning, I foresaw all the time I was stuck doing this just until lunch—forty-five minutes to go. Ugh. "Ah well," I thought, "come lunch I'll be able to chill and enjoy myself and escape all this focus." (If I couldn't escape the concrete slab physically, I could do so mentally.)

But my mind wasn't having it and retorted with, "Where are you going to 'escape'? Your boring, quiet room?" This wasn't a health club class that I could leave behind for home and the entertainment of Internet and movies. I was on a mountain.

My thought continued, "Plus, even when lunch comes, you'll soon be faced with the afternoon session—and after it, an evening session. Come bedtime, you get to look forward to the 5:15 wake-up call and the glorious day all over again."

Seeing what I got myself into up on this mountain, I then did the next logical thing and looked ahead to four days from now. Yeah, then I'd go back down into town and..... "and what, Brandon?" again my mind interrupted itself. "Watch TV? Surf the net? Plus, what will all this looking ahead make of your meantime here?"

I paused.

"Wake up, Brandon. You came all this way to experience this, and now you're thinking about when you get to leave?!"

This art that required total presence had my mind on the run from it. This wasn't ironic, but indicative that I was in the right place. Tai chi was slamming the living present right into my face. How a subtle art like it can slam anything is a wonder, but I realized I had better get comfortable with the here and now and the slow repetitive movements. It was all a bit of a downer—like an acceptance of defeat—yet was also the beginning of a practice that helped lessen the trap of living in the past, living for the future, or being wrapped up in present thought.

I'd live and witness the lifestyle here, inspiring my own growth and appreciation for the richness of this practice and life overall.

The Life

Days started at 5:15 a.m. My alarm rang, and I awoke looking forward not just to fighting sleep but countering it head-on with a jog about three-quarters of a mile up the mountain road and back. If I timed it right, I'd run with the other students. After getting back, it was twenty minutes of stretches and calisthenics. This included hopping from one end of the concrete slab to the other from a squatted position. After about six of these jumps, your legs are feeling it. After fifteen, you're wanting a break. After the twenty-five I needed to complete the task, there was significant leg burn. These were followed up with a crouched jog. Then it was high kicks from one end to the other, followed by punches. After warm-ups, we dove into the actual tai chi session.

I did the routine my trainer taught me, but I was also taught a couple others. One was demonstrated in the picture above. Simply twist your trunk back and forth (left to right to left) while having both arms out. One hand is higher than the other with palm up while the lower hand has palm down. Hands switch roles when twisting the opposite way. Some other students did similar tai chi; others worked on longer, more varied choreography that I'd get to later. Then others practiced kung fu with sword or long stick.

All of this took place with a backdrop appropriate to inspire an art devoted to clear mind and presence.

After sessions we'd break for meals. Food was a mix of locally grown vegetables and greens and usually a meat and bread. We had duck once or twice. Once I prepared eggs for everybody by scrambling fifteen or so in the wok mixed with vegetables. Students took turns cooking and doing the dishes.

We also had a break after lunch from about one o'clock to two-thirty. This, I'd come to find, was nap time. And it wasn't just the others here indicating this by taking naps themselves: my own physiology was loud and clear. Being here was like hitting the reset button on my body. Minus the stimulation of media, sweets, caffeine, and social outings, and with the added focus of our practice, I became keenly aware of what my body needed and when. And after lunch, I needed to shut my eyes. So I did for about half hour. Combined with my physiological clarity was a mental calm that allowed for the best reading of my life. I flew through and soaked in the thought-provoking non-fiction I had purchased from street sales mom and son in Beijing.

When I didn't read, I might walk down to where most of the other students stayed. I discovered their lodging the first day when I peeked over the edge of the concrete platform upon hearing voices coming from below.

I had been standing on their roof.

Walking to the left and down some concrete steps, I grabbed a spare shovel and thought to help. But it turned out that even for something so benign (so I assumed) as shoveling, I was taken to task. The trainer down there—a trainer-in-making, thirtyish brute of a guy with a thick tuft of hair and the start of the master's beard—interrupted my work to show me how to do it right. He secured the shovel and blurted, "Ha!"—the shovel prepared for battle; "whoo!"—it was thrust into the dirt pile; and "hwa!"—it removed with a load of earth.

I don't think he was being funny, either.

Seeing this wasn't all that surprising—it was a tai chi school. But just the same, it provided a striking example of taking this ordinary chore and perfecting it. The trainer didn't think about how to get it done faster or easier, but how to get it done *better*—being present and honing the kinetics. He focused on all the movement involved in the simple shovel thrust—the upright torso, the curve and twist of each arm, the bent knees—the body as a temple of energy.

I took back the shovel and tried, and I revealed the same difficulties I had on top of the concrete platform. I wasn't used to thinking about form, but function. "You got a bigger shovel and wheelbarrow?" I thought. I was ignorant of the fact that maybe here the task wasn't about the accomplishment.

During their leisure time, the students would put down the shovels. Some might pick up a stick or sword and practice routines. But they'd also just talk or play a game.

The bottom left shows the student-trainer who took me to shovel school.

This day, the student-trainer continued his practice into break time; he'd have a student step on his lower back while he split and leaned forward.

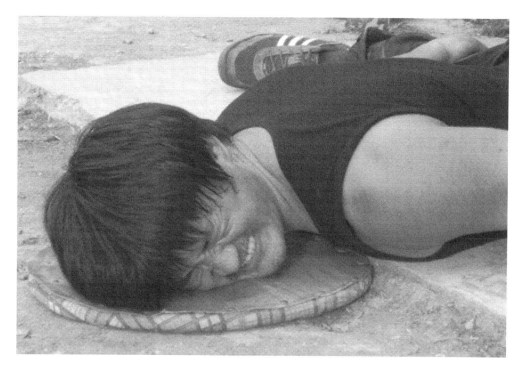

He would also regularly do handstands against a building with fists against the concrete. He was pretty intense.

At dusk, a group would sometimes go for a walk. Once I tagged along as they went along the road up the mountain, and once again when they walked down it. In both instances I was introduced to some humble homesteads occupied by neighbors contented with the quiet life up here. One was an old woman gardener from whom the school bought vegetables. Another was a husband, wife, and young son.

A couple of the nights everyone congregated on the porch of the main cabin. The headmaster played his erhu or woodwind.

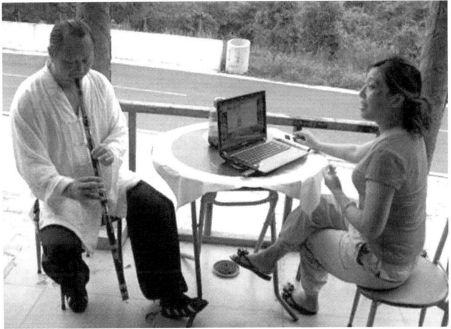

As you might suspect, the music and the scenery provided a sensory feast—exaggerated given the mind-body training we exercised that day.

Some sang along.

Others sat and listened.

Spirits were high.

I planned on living the martial arts lifestyle for just the four days and three nights. Though not long, this whole new environment—one that encouraged the focus of every moment, no less—meant a concentrated, super-saturated seventy-two-plus hours. With little to no English spoken at the school, I was known not as Brandon Ferdig, but Feng Xiang, a man more comfortable with the present and in not needing snacks or TV or Internet or some other stimulus to be content. Whether as motivation ("Only five more minutes!") or complaint ("I'll never get out of here!"), my thoughts of time decreased during practice—slowing down the movement of my arms and upper body with the gliding, trunk twists right to left. Yet for all the infinity within those four days, I knew I was only scratching the surface—just chipping away at the shell of a constant, racing mind, revealing a calm that I wanted a bigger taste of. It wasn't free to stay, though. If there were only some way I could work off the expense...

Round Two

I had asked a couple fellow students and trainers about their interest in working on their English, and on day three the headmaster offered me a reduced rate if I agreed to teach English to fellow tai chi students. I graciously accepted, bid farewell to previous brainstorms to see the Muslim and Tibetan populated areas of western China, and stared at another five days of tai chi, kung fu, and calm.

I considered this round two of my training. And this time the headmaster took me a little more under his wing.

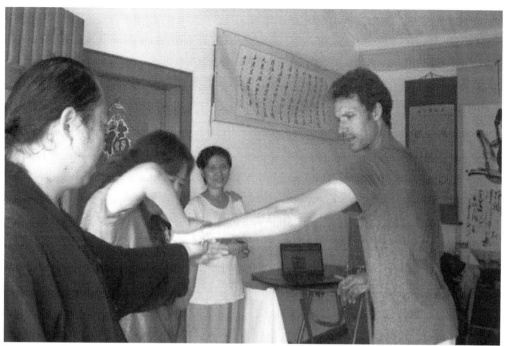

He liked to show off a bit at the goading of some others by playing with the newbies.

I think I held my own.

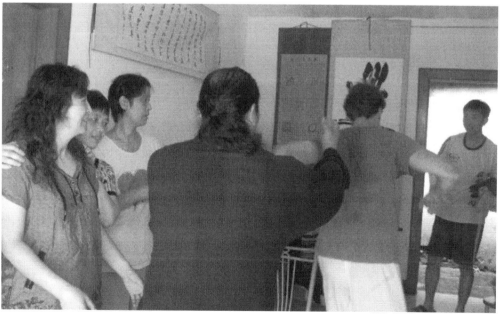

Had him right where I wanted.

I should note that this guy was the real deal. He'd won all sorts of competitions and used to work with action star Jackie Chan. He looked hefty, even a bit out of shape, but that was an illusion. He was a brick.

While he schooled me, I spent an hour twice a day teaching three regular English students: the twelve and nineteen-year-old girls and a twenty-six-year-old guy—my roommate who arrived the day I decided to extend my stay. In our thin, loose martial arts attire we'd sit in chairs in my roommate's and my room and practice conversations, vocabulary, and writing. The tutoring was aided by the younger girl having some English textbooks from her regular school. Teaching English: the job that opened the door to all of China, now allowed me this chance to teach here—all so I could be a student on the concrete slab.

My experience as a teacher also helped me to relate better to the student-trainer's frustrations on account of my struggles. Since I had now picked up a couple basic tai chi movements, he started me with the more involved choreography. I was having real trouble with it, however, struggling to remember even a few consecutive movements. While I was already feeling pressure and some embarrassment about my difficulty, he added to it by shaking his head and laughing in a disbelieving, "Are you stupid?" kind of way. I wanted to react in a "screw you" kind of way. But like a good tai chi student, I let the reactive part of me come and go and was actually able to empathize with the guy.

I recalled my own difficulty months earlier as a teacher. I had this student who just couldn't get it. He'd try to read aloud what we had just reviewed in detail, but would do so making sounds that weren't close to what was written. I would run my fingers through my hair. "C'mon!" I would think (and one time even said out loud, I regret to say.)

Here at the tai chi school, my trainer probably wasn't used to dealing with foreigners having such difficulty. Discerning this, I went from defensive to understanding. I asked my nearby roommate, whose English was good, to tell my trainer, "I know how hard it is to teach me. I know how hard it is to teach someone who doesn't get it. I'm sorry I'm such a hard student to teach." The trainer received the translated message, and I watched his face soften. He then put his hand on my shoulder with a reassuring smile. I glimpsed the point at which emotions that separate people (my feeling insulted and him losing patience) contend with ones that connect (compassion, understanding).

I blame my struggles on my difficulty going from my head to my body, from recollection to action. You have to simply do without thinking laboriously (similar to learning a language or salsa dancing). Making it trickier, though, the gradual movements in tai chi—at least as it was practiced here—make proper posture a challenge as you have to hold strenuous poses. And the smooth movement reveals any and all mistakes.

During practice, I kept trying to memorize every angle of every pose, every maneuver of every limb. With two arms, two legs, and a trunk and head, that's five or six different things that I tried to be conscious of simultaneously. Impossible. I learned up on that mountain the importance of getting out of the analytical and into the flow of being. This is what my peers were so much better at than I.

Watch and Learn

On my fourth day, my roommate arrived. His English name was Bruce, and he was a body builder from Chongqing. His frame was a muscular 5'9" (175cm), but despite his athleticism, I had a three-day head start on the guy. Thus, I assumed I'd have someone to learn the moves with—if not gain from by showing him a thing or two. Fast forward two days later, and the headmaster assigned Bruce to help me in learning the moves.

From the first day when I met the gang shoveling dirt, to the everyday practice on the concrete slab, I was struck by how kinetic everyone was.

Perfect movement was their quest.

They'd spend minutes on end on a single movement the way I might spend that time perfecting a paragraph.

When I did attain sufficient familiarity over the simpler choreography, I didn't have to think about the movement and could just be and feel it. From that vantage point, I glimpsed some powerful stillness. I'm betting the others here attained more than glimpses.

I'd like to believe that learning went both ways. One afternoon, some of us students walked down into the valley forests to gather firewood and kindling for the kitchen stove. Down along the woodsy trail, my nineteen-year-old English student had a problem bagging a pile of twigs and pine needles. She thought to remedy the issue of cut hands by taking two five-foot-long sticks to pinch and lift the pile. She wasn't getting too far, though, just as I don't when eating rice with chopsticks. I noticed two rake-like tools sitting there and grabbed them and motioned to her, "Allow me." I bundled that stick/needle salad with my "tongs" and then compressed and hoisted a generous amount into the bag.

"So clever, Feng Xiang" she said.

"Ah shucks," I thought. "I just eat different, that's all."

At the end, we bundled our gathered logs. We needed a tight packing to secure them together up the narrow and hilly path. Student-Trainer found vines that worked as string, but jutting branches still had to be snapped off or else they'd catch brush on the way back. One stubby branch was proving troublesome despite the kung fu trained kicking the men were attacking it with. I noticed a large rock and wedged it under the branch to construct a crude lever, and the force of my undisciplined, less-effective kick was enough to snap it. This move gained me a few more grateful recipients of my "clever"ness. I was actually pretty happy to be able to contribute something.

From landscaping to lumberjacking, these guys first thought of how to better use their bodies. I looked for alternatives to my body. These are generalizations, of course, but in the big picture we see trends, and in the individual people and individual examples we see illustrations. I couldn't help but wonder whether our solutions here exemplified the development of the East and the West. While the East perfected the punch, the West perfected the gun. The historic isolation of the world's peoples allowed them to hone their culture and strengths. This quaint display in the woods, and of my stay overall, revealed the benefits in store when we learn from each other.

***

Wu Dang Shan Temples: Fantasy in Reality

Though much tradition was supplanted in twentieth century China, there still remains activity tied to days far gone. Not only was I exposed to a 400-year-old martial art, but also I witnessed a ceremonial custom held within buildings dating back to times far earlier than tai chi. Revealed here was a line where the past and the present, and the artistic and the real, were beautifully interwoven.

One day, without ever saying why, the somewhat-bilingual girlfriend of the headmaster strongly encouraged me to come along with other students and teachers. Once again this year, I was clueless but curious. I agreed, and a bus picked us up, transported us up the curvy mountain road, and dropped us off at a large parking lot. The lot was surrounded by fake-old architecture that housed restaurants, convenience stores, tourist shops, and a sword store. This was also where my tai chi school's home temple was. We walked across the lot past all the stores and up the stone walk to the temple, a sizable complex working its way up the mountain.

I wandered around and inside some of the buildings.

Straight out of a movie, isn't it?

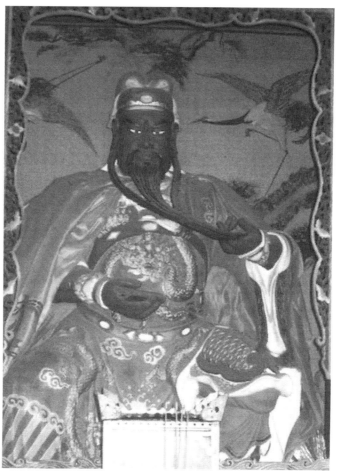

Gathered outside on the main level was a crowd that didn't look typically tourist. With their high-end cameras, I took them to be reporters. Then, to their anticipation but my surprise, Master started putting on a tai chi kung fu show.

After his brief performance before flashes and claps, he put on an elegant, navy blue robe and asked the rest of us to join in for group shots.

Master, myself, and my three English students

This was all just a prelude.

Master donned a black cap and asked everyone to ascend the two flights of the temple complex's stone steps. At the top was a decorative building and altar within.

Master and others prepared for a ceremonial "graduation." (I'm not sure of the term because as much a destination for this student, it was a recognition of her next level of training.) Master started off the ceremony by lighting some incense.

Then he turned and addressed the pupil.

Other masters looked on.

Master then stepped aside to allow for the teacher she would be working under.

The ceremony continued with some sort of shoe tradition.

Along with this activity were resonant "boonnggssss" from a stately, cool bronze bell. The press snapped shots regularly, adding flashes and noises that took from the moment. Nonetheless, it was a solemn and proud event.

Afterward, there were more opportunities for photos in front of the ceremony building.

Concluding the afternoon, we all went to one of those restaurants pictured below to celebrate:

Typical family style dining. Also typical, the food was great.

Surprising to me, though, these guys drank.

Even in the act of pouring a beverage that will make you loose, they perform the pour with iron grip focus.

On another occasion, circumstances were similar minus the ceremony. We headed up the mountain, walked to the temple, and the group greeted more cameras with some classic poses.

The Spaniard in the back left attended a sister school.

But this time, Master and his star pupil (the student-trainer at the school) performed a duo routine fit for film.

Their show was a culmination not just of their own ten to twenty years of training, but of the culture's centuries.

The outfits, the ceremony, the temple, and of course, the art brought all these elements together as well as past years to the present. I half-wondered what year it actually was.

The whole setting felt so much like a fairytale. For the locals, though, these fairytales maintain the arts and customs still pronounced in everyday life.

Finally on this second visit there was yet another wrinkle in this continuum and interplay of reality and art.

Why recreate in a movie studio what is already built right here?

As the cast and crew assembled, I investigated.

It's a good bet that when you watch TV in China, you'll find a period piece from one of two eras: either these old days of imperial China or a story of China's fight against the Japanese in the 1930s.

I don't even know how to express the strange ball of yarn that was the real actors on this set versus the actors of the real show during the ceremony, the cameramen depicting reality in this movie versus the cameramen capturing reality in the ceremony. Even without all that, there's the living history of these temple walls housing ancient-to-present-day customs and the demonstration of past ways for present-day audiences to relive. I guess I can say that these occasions on Wu Dang Shan were all a bit *sur*real, adding to my understanding of Chinese culture yesterday and today.

***

I left Wu Dang Shan the following afternoon and rode back down to the village at the foot of the mountain. I could feel the air warm up the bus as we descended. I hopped in a taxi at the bus station and returned to the apartment/hotel that boarded me my first night. The next morning I woke up early, a habit by now from the nine days prior and one I intended to keep practicing. It wasn't as easy as it had become at the school. For someone typically turned off by rules and group mentality, I appreciated the power of a team regulated for synchronicity as it influenced me to new heights. Without the daily structure, sleeping in was much more tempting. But I got up.

The town of Wu Dang Shan was a fitting place to take this practice back into civilization. The town shared an identity with the mountain and the traditions established atop it. As I jogged along a stone walkway toward a large, open town square, I discovered I wasn't the only one starting the day this way. Others were working solo or in a group. I found a good place and did the stretches, kicks, and then a routine of tai chi choreography. It was hard to finish it right, resisting the temptation to shave a few moves off the end and call it quits a little early. But when I did finish properly, I saw the town and all around me with a different set of eyes. The clarity, calm, objectivity, and presence with which I walked away from the town square that morning had me thinking, "This is right; I want every moment of my life to be from this perspective."

Later that day, I hopped on the train and said goodbye to Wu Dang Shan. This would be the last major event for me in China before returning home to Minnesota.

Chapter Eighteen: Heading Home

I took another sleeper car to Xi'an. There is over a week's worth of sites to see here. But my extended stay at Wu Dang Shan meant I had to go right to the airport to fly back to Guangzhou.

Then from Guangzhou, I took the same bus route to Zhuhai I had taken eleven months earlier. Like my whole year, the remaining two days in Zhuhai (and China) were split between travel and domestic mindsets. One demanded I clear out my apartment, pack up my things, sell what I couldn't take with me, and go to the bank and cash out my account. The other part had me soak in these last moments, reflect on my year, and then say goodbye to places and people.

On my final afternoon, I walked to the same place I had my first morning: the docks.

Taken that first morning in Zhuhai.

The day before this shot, I arrived to China fresh, not knowing what to expect. I simply exited the plane with my pre-conceived notions of hectic traffic, lots of people, and smog. Thankfully, these stereotypes weren't too common. I anticipated a year of boundless travel and exploratory possibilities in that way you make loose plans to do things "in the next six months." It's exciting as you really can do *any*thing, but realize (hopefully) sooner rather than later that you can't do *every*thing. Time to buckle down...sort of.

After taking in the activity of the docks on this last afternoon, these two unknowingly saw me off wonderfully:

That evening I had a goodbye dinner with fellow teachers and former students—all of them new friends.

My roomie Ralf on the floor, then left to right: Marilyn, Jerry, Emily the teacher, Emily the accountant hill-climber, and Sally the TPR employee.

I left the following morning on an unusually clear, warm, sunny day. In her VW Beetle, Lucy drove me to the Zhuhai airport. The ride forty-five minutes southwest of my neighborhood featured lush green palm trees and bright blue skies that lit up the brand-new housing developments being erected along the highway. "I don't remember Zhuhai being so beautiful," I thought as I looked out the window. This actually added to the already-sad spirit in which I left, knowing that this eleven-month Asian era of my life—and with it the teaching, socializing, traveling, and relationships—was now done and soon gone.

I wanted to hold these moments like a parent wishing their toddler would never get big; acknowledging the obvious—that moments can't be held, just experienced—was difficult. I had to accept that situations are created and occur, never to occur again. That's the sad and beautiful reality.

I flew to Shanghai. After a couple hours in that gigantic airport, I left China on the day my visa expired. While still grounded, now on a United States airline to Chicago, it started to feel like America already. Compared with the flight I had just taken hours before, the attendants now were older, heavier, and grumpier. Later, I'd also find that the food wasn't as good.

Lastly, it was a jaunt in the air from Chicago to Minneapolis. I was home.

Jerald, my older brother who dropped me off nearly a year earlier, picked me up from MSP airport. I saw his car approach and his face behind the wheel. (What do you say when you haven't seen someone in a while? There's always that neat reunion vibe.) Driving out to his house in Buffalo, Minnesota, it struck me how everything looked the same back here in the Twin Cities. China was always building. Jerald responded that China is developing and America is developed. I suppose he's right, but in the coming days and weeks, I'd feel the lack of growth-energy here in America.

A box of Grape Nuts, which I had missed in China, was waiting for me on the kitchen counter at Jerald's house. I had a bowl that night and stayed up much too late since it felt like afternoon to my China bio-clock. I then got up from my "nap" at 5 a.m. and walked out of the house to begin my tai chi routine.

Chapter Nineteen: Life Learned

Impressed with China

Days before I left to go to China a politically left-leaning friend of mine said he was interested to see if my own political views might change while there. His angle was, "Yeah, they're Communist, but look at their impressive education and transportation projects. We could learn from them." Some popular media in the United States had offered similar takes.

Then there were the detractors.

A couple other friends told me to watch out because the government could, and does, arrest and imprison people for small, unpredictable reasons. "Don't do or say anything they might not like," they'd tell me. A friend of mine who taught in China spoke with displeasure about her experience including her mail being opened and *People* magazines confiscated.

Not settled into any "pro" or "anti" camp, I left for China.

Right away upon my arrival, I was surprised to see people seeming so peaceful and content. All year long I'd feel safe in the city. I immediately saw signs of legal and social freedom not present back in America.

Then a few weeks went by.

My blog was censored. I went to perform a transaction at the bank, and it took all day and cost me unanticipated fees. My mail was opened. I saw a people complicit with what I considered to be restrictive government policy. I saw an unkempt population who thoughtlessly threw plastic, Styrofoam, and glass into the ocean.

I felt both sides of the anti/pro China views weigh on me. Depending on the time of year would determine which way I swayed. But overall, I learned that I was *impressed* with China. The good parts were impressed upon me; the bad parts were as well. And as such, the truth was deepened.

I realized the pull to take a side on any given issue, and subsequently, head down into the depths of an allegiance—people look for such drama of "terrible" or "great." But traveling and living there wasn't about defining a position. It was about getting to know my world better.

***

Letting Go; Letting Life

After getting home, I looked back on the moments of my year unfettered by any of the concerns I had during the experiences themselves. I may have been nervous and uncomfortable onstage for the Chinese New Year Celebration, and I may have been frustrated when my beautiful musical companion admitted to having a fiancé, but recalling these with this hindsight advantage provided the benefit of recognizing them for just what they were: precious.

Demonstrating American cuisine, I cooked an omelet at the TPR food festival.

Also looking back, I realized how little I had to do with creating these situations. I didn't plan them or direct these people together. I didn't go to China with any ideas of modeling for a school's brochures or cooking in front of an audience. (I actually did try to go to China to model before discovering this teaching opportunity but was rejected.)

It was that which is outside of me—the people, the circumstances—that was most responsible for these opportunities. All I did was avail myself to that which life brought me and then injected myself where best served—teaching, posing. I *was* able to be creative in my pursuits such as asking around to see if fellow tai chi students wanted to learn English and thus enabling my stay at Wu Dang Shan. But such manipulation, I realized, was predicated by the fact that life offered these circumstances in the first place by combining factors in ways I had no ability to foresee— i.e. my English teaching opening the door to study tai chi.

I think this is the delicate dance of self versus "other" that has been written about and defined differently from every corner of the world for all documented human history. Religious people define this outside factor as God. Atheists reject the existence of it at all. I don't know what "it" is, but seeing it in action repeatedly throughout my year, I've come to recognize it as a reliable source for new and amazing experiences around each corner. My time in China taught me to stretch my travel lifestyle of staying alert, available, and open over the span of eleven months. Since returning home, I've tried to keep it going.

Naturally, a domesticated life hasn't allowed for such concentrated movement and variety as my time in China. But such established efforts invested in career and long-term relationships fulfill a different need for personal and professional growth, and I've learned that the drama and excitement of life doesn't end with responsibilities, occupation, age, or domesticity. I think excitement ends when I use these factors as excuses to overfeed my hunger of activity and adventure with the food of vicarious existence—living solely through others or television.

I love travel, but I don't need to wait for my next departure to let go and let life—let go of the burdens, participate in whichever way I am inspired to do so, and soak in every precious moment along the way.

Thank you

Words

I want to thank: book editors Leah Cochenet Noel, Rondi Feyereisen, and Book Architects for helping get this book into shape; The Loft Literary Center in Minneapolis for providing guidance through one of their great courses and then Sandy, Deb, and Carol for our subsequent writer's group; novelist Elizabeth Stoever for being my teammate on this road to authorship by reading each others' manuscripts; Nick Rosener of Technick Consulting for creative direction; and previous editors who've help shape my writing (Lisa Hickey, Doug Tice, Eric Ringham, Justin Cascio, Phil Pina, and Craig Westover.)

Appearance/Technical

I want to thank: photographer Jessica Mealey for helping me with image design; videographer Keith Porter for helping me edit the footage (for the Vook); Spring Chen for voicing the audio segments(for the Vook); Minneapolis Telecommunications Network for technical support (for the Vook); and Alan Pranke for cover design.

Opportunity

I want to thank TPR English Academy of Zhuhai for providing me with the opportunity to come to China. This was the seed that blossomed into this book. I want to thank all my friends and colleagues in Zhuhai for your support and wisdom throughout the year.

Family and Friends

I want to thank: my big brother, Jerald and his wife Maggie, not just for rides to the airport, but for a place to stay when transitioning between travel and for a place to work on this book; my little brother, Joseph, for reading me the manuscript out loud; Mom and Dad for constant encouragement; and friends Gary, Dan, Ryan, Paul, Dan, and Natalie for providing moral support through this process.

Financial

I want to thank: all thirty-four donors who chipped in to my Kickstarter campaign for this book project; my employers (Minneapolis School District, Teacher's On Call, Teaching Temps, Pinstripes restaurant, and Griffin Recovery Enterprises) while I wrote this book so I could eat and pay rent.

Finally, I want to thank you for reading my book.